CABBAGETOWN
REMEMBERED

GEORGE H. RUST-D'EYE

Stoddart

A BOSTON MILLS PRESS BOOK

CANADIAN CATALOGUING IN PUBLICATION DATA

Rust-D'Eye, George 1944-
  Cabbagetown remembered

ISBN 0-919783-00-7

1. Toronto (Ont.)-Social life and customs.   2. Toronto (Ont.)-
History.   I. Title

FC3097.52.R9 1984   971.3'541   C84-098872-9
F1059.5.T686C35 1984

Published by Stoddart Publishing Co. Limited, 1993
34 Lesmill Road
Toronto,Canada
M3B 2T6
(416) 445-3333

A BOSTON MILLS PRESS BOOK
The Boston Mills Press
132 Main Street
Erin, Ontario
N0B IT0
(519) 833-2407

Winners of the
Heritage Canada
Communications Award

American Association
for State and Local History
Award Winner

Design by Gillian Stead
Typeset by Linotext, Toronto
Printed in Canada by Ampersand Printing

The publisher gratefully acknowledges the support of the Canada Council,
Ontario Ministry of Culture and Communications, Ontario Arts Council
and Ontario Publishing Centre in the development of writing and publishing in Canada.

DEDICATION

This book is dedicated to Gordon Sinclair, who was born on June 3, 1900 at 375 Carlton Street, within earshot of the howling of wolves at the Riverdale Zoo.

He rejoiced in and nurtured a self-claimed reputation as a curmudgeon, and as a man who didn't care what the public thought about him. Yet, upon news of his death, on May 17th, 1984, heartfelt tributes poured in from far and wide. For Gordon Sinclair's strength of personality, his generosity of soul, and his ability to express exactly what he thought, had brought him international respect and immense popularity. Even those who violently disagreed with what he said would not miss the opportunity to hear him say it.

Like Cabbagetown, Gordon Sinclair was real and unique —a beloved Canadian institution. He is greatly missed.

G.H.R

George H. Rust D'Eye, the author of *Cabbagetown Remembered* is a local resident of Cabbagetown, a Torontonian by birth and a lawyer by profession. He is a former metropolitan solicitor for the Municipality of Metropolitan Toronto. He is now a partner in the firm Weir and Foulds, practicing primarily in the field of municipal law.

Mr. Rust D'Eye is a former chairman of the Toronto Historical Board, of which he was a member for 13 years. He is a former president of the Don Vale Association of Homeowners and Residents. He has published a number of articles in *Seven News* relating to the history of Ward 7. He is also an avid photographer, speaker, walking tour guide and collector of books and documents relating to the history of Toronto and heritage preservation.

AUTHOR'S PREFACE

The last quarter of the nineteenth century, a period during which the population of Toronto increased from 69,000 to over 200,000, saw the publication of a number of "view books". The best known of these were 'Illustrated, Toronto, Past and Present', by J. Timperlake (1877), 'Toronto Past and Present', by C. Pelham Mulvany (1884), 'Toronto, Old and New', by G. Mercer Adam (1891), and 'Artwork on Toronto', published by W.H. Carre and Co. (1898). The general approach and purpose of the writers of these works is best summed up in the following quote from the preface to 'Illustrated Toronto, Past and Present':

> "Toronto being the largest, wealthiest and most important city in the Province of Ontario, it is desirable that its rapid growth, wealth and advantages as a commercial city, should be known amongst its citizens and visitors."

Profusely illustrated with views of the most important parks, streets, houses, institutions and commercial houses, these books celebrated the growth of the 'Queen City of the West', paying homage to the "men of substance and character" who were responsible for its "phenomenal success".

Such books, of course, never referred to or acknowledged the existence of Cabbagetown or the people who dwelt within its precincts. Emphasis on the contributions of capital and personal leadership to the growth of Toronto left virtually nothing to be said about the city's more humble inhabitants who provided its labour. In contrast to the thousands of "views" taken of the homes and business places of the rich, almost no early photographs of the original Cabbagetown can be found. Only with the development of public social welfare schemes early in this century, did any body of information and pictorial documentation of conditions in Cabbagetown and the other "slum", the Ward, begin to accumulate.

Drawing upon this latter body of material, on the available historical records relating to the businesses and institutions of Cabbagetown, and on the recollections of its "old-timers", this book is intended to remedy, in some small way, the imbalance of attention to the lower social orders and their environment, caused by the perspective of the early writers on the history of this city.

While the subject-matter of this book contrasts sharply with that of the Victorian commentaries referred to above, it owes much to them in its style. This is deliberate. The history of Cabbagetown and its people lends itself ideally to the parochial approach of those early observers of the development of Toronto. Similarly, the fact that so few important events or radical changes occurred in this area during the middle period of its history, makes necessary the piecemeal encyclopaedic treatment which characterized some of the early writings on the city. Thus, the concentration of attention on this area is not intended to convey that Cabbagetown was in all ways unique, nor that its history is totally unrelated to its local and national environment. Rather, it is intended in this writing to reflect the perspectives of those who lived in Cabbagetown, and to describe the characteristics of their life experience as a component of the urban fabric.

This book was written in conjunction with the Cabbagetown Local History Project, co-ordinated by the Parliament Street Branch of the Toronto Public Library. Following the initiative of Julie Hale and Keith Stratten, staff members of that branch, the project commenced work in November, 1981 with the hiring of Jean Wright to co-ordinate the workers and organize the many volunteer contributions which began to flow in from past and present residents of the area, some of whom had lived in Cabbagetown since before the turn of the century.

Space limitations prevent the acknowledgement in this preface of all of those who contributed time and effort in making the Cabbagetown Local History Project a success. However, special mention must be made of the work of William Hambly and James Ealey, old-time Cabbagetowners whose reminiscences and research contributed so much to the store of information which the project accumulated. Another volunteer, Pat Hay, researched churches. Her work was so well done that her historical summary on Sacred Heart Church was incorporated almost word-for-word into the book. Jean Wright's excellent and tireless work as Co-ordinator of the project must also be acknowledged, together with that of Colleen Kelly. Both of them contributed greatly to making the author's work much easier and more enjoyable. Thanks also must go to Marjorie Hand and Isobel Gill, who worked in the administration of the project, and to the students and staff of Eastdale Collegiate for their participation in it.

The contributions of Learnxs Foundation, Sony of Canada, BGM Colour Laboratories, the Province of Ontario Career Action Programme and the Ontario Heritage Foundation are also gratefully acknowledged.

Some of the photographs came from private sources. Others were obtained from the City of Toronto Archives, the Province of Ontario Archives, and the Baldwin Room, Metropolitan Toronto Library.

Many historical sources were consulted in the research and preparation for the book. Some of the most useful publications are listed in the bibliography. In this respect, special reference must be made to the writings of Hugh Garner, Gordon Sinclair, J.V. McAree and William Hambly, whose published works on their early lives in Cabbagetown and vicinity provide so much valuable information on what it was like to live there in the early days.

To all of the above, to the countless others who made contributions to the project and to Gemma Trott, who typed the manuscript, go the author's thanks.

Queen Street East across the Don, near Broadview
— From a postcard, Circa 1908

INTRODUCTION
WHERE IS CABBAGETOWN

Cabbagetown is where you find it. It has never been a legally-defined place name, nor was it ever surveyed. In fact the question of where Cabbagetown is—or was—is the subject of considerable controversy, even among people who lived in it during the same period of time as each other.

Of the best-known Cabbagetown historians, few accept the earliest and most restrictive definition—the area bounded by Gerrard Street on the north, Dundas Street on the south, Parliament Street on the west, and the Don River on the east. In fact, few of them accept what any of the others accepts.

J.V. McAree, whose autobiography, *Cabbagetown Store,* is considered by many to describe most accurately the spirit which was Cabbagetown, states:

> The word was applied to that part of Toronto lying south of Gerrard Street, north of Queen and east from Parliament Street to the Don.
>
> Claims to have been old citizens of Cabbagetown put forth in later years by persons living beyond these boundaries have been properly disallowed and resented.[1]

Hugh Garner, the tough-talking author of the novel *Cabbagetown,* describes the locality in these words:

> Toronto's Cabbagetown remains only a memory to those of us who lived in it when it was a slum. Less than half a mile long and even narrower from north to south, it was situated in the east-central part of the city, its boundaries being Parliament Street on the west, Gerrard Street on the north, the Don River on the east and Queen Street on the south. To the west of Parliament Street was and is Moss Park, a neighbourhood now the temporary home or lighting place of a more transient type of slum-dweller. This neighbourhood is sometimes referred to as Cabbagetown, as is the area north of Gerrard Street, but this is an error.[2]

This would appear to be the most popular definition of Cabbagetown among those who lived in it before the Second World War. However, the oldest living Cabbagetown historian, W.B. (Bill) Hambly, born in 1896, has this to say:

> I believe, however, that Cabbage Town is that part of the city east of Sherbourne Street, and south of Winchester Street, because this is where the people claim the Cabbage Town tradition.[3]

This is the most expansive of the descriptions of Cabbagetown accepted by "old-timers", and comes closest to accommodating the recent tendency to apply the name to the area north of Gerrard Street, which was previously almost universally accepted as the northern boundary of Cabbagetown. Modern-day Torontonians seem to have no hesitation in using the name "Cabbagetown" for assorted parts of the City in a way which would make McAree, Garner, Hambly and their contemporaries cringe. Not only do the presently-accepted boundaries not coincide with the historical ones, but some of them entirely exclude the area south of Gerrard.[4]

The above discussion points up a major difficulty involved in trying to define "Cabbagetown". The answer may depend on the approach. A strictly historical inquiry will turn up one set of boundaries; a reference to the Cabbagetown "tradition" yields another; and resort to the common acceptances of to-day will produce a third. And yet too many people feel too strongly about Cabbagetown simply to let subjectivity govern and dismiss the pronouncements of the old-timers as not having any present relevance to the issue. Whatever the significance of the recent relatively short-term application of the term to areas totally different in geography and quality of life from the original Cabbagetown, (wherever it may have been), it is not enough to say that Cabbagetown is a state of mind. One must ask: "Whose mind?" and "When?". If there is a "Cabbagetown tradition", and there certainly appears to be one, what are its characteristics, and does it exist to-day, or has the word simply been borrowed and applied without reference to history?

This book is concerned generally with the history of the area of Toronto south of Bloor street between Sherbourne Street and the Don. This fact, however, is not intended to imply an acceptance of the recent tendency by members of the real estate industry and other to apply the name Cabbagetown to parts of Toronto for which it is totally inappropriate, such as some blocks of Sherbourne Street, or Castle Frank Cresent, let alone Jarvis Street or areas east of the Don. However, as will be seen, there are a number of unifying factors which make this area appropriate for historical study separate from other parts of the city. Also, it would appear to be the widest general area for which the description "Cabbagetown" may have some claim to validity, and in which a search for the "real" Cabbagetown may prove fruitful.

It is intended in this short book to highlight historical and social developments in this area from the earliest days of English-speaking settlement up to the beginning of the Second World War. The history of "Cabbagetown" since that time is a story in itself. Also, the recent history of the area, fairly well documented, has involved, of course, the destruction of much of the physical and social fabric of what was once the heart of Cabbagetown. Finally, much of the content of this historical account is based on the memories of those who lived through the "golden years of Cabbagetown" and the subsequent War and Depression, people to whom "Cabbagetown" has a profound meaning, bearing very little relationship to the brass coach lamps and sandblasted brick which act as hallmarks of the Cabbagetown of to-day.

WHERE IT STARTED

The roots of Cabbagetown, and, indeed, of the City of Toronto, can be traced back to a small English settlement established in 1793 at the waterfront not far from where the Don River enters the Bay.

A previous French presence in Toronto had all but disappeared with the burning of Fort Rouillé in 1759. In 1787, Lord Dorchester, (Sir Guy Carleton), governor-in-chief of the then Province of Quebec, arranged the purchase from the Mississauga Indians of 250,880 acres of land having a frontage of 14 miles on the Lake Ontario shoreline east from the Humber River, and to a distance of 28 miles to the north. The transaction, known as the Toronto Purchase, was consummated at the Carrying Place of the Bay of Quinte, near present-day Trenton. The price: £1700, and 249 barrels of cloth, axes and odds and ends "dear to the heart of the simple savage". A later agreement, in 1805, formally settled the boundaries of the English acquisition.

This area was originally included in the Nassau District, (1788), then in the Township of Dublin in the District of Toronto after the creation of Upper Canada, in 1791; and then became part of the Home District, in 1792. In 1791, John Graves Simcoe, a veteran of the American revolutionary war, was appointed first lieutenant-governor of Upper Canada. He arrived at Quebec on November 11, 1791 and proceeded to establish the first seat of government for the new province at Newark (now Niagara-on-the-Lake). However, the proximity of that site to American soil caused him to look for other areas not quite so vulnerable to sudden attack.

Previous exploration and surveying of the Toronto area and harbour convinced Simcoe that this would be an excellent location for a garrison. At that time the harbour was protected by a peninsula creating a defensible channel at its west end, which Simcoe called Gibraltar Point. It wasn't until 1858 that the washing out of an eastern channel by a storm cut off the former peninsula, creating what we now know as the Toronto Island.

Lieutenant-Governor Simcoe felt that the site of Toronto was the best location in the province for a naval arsenal, and wanted to build his ships there. However, it was not his original intention to establish a town, let alone make it his new capital, which he proposed to establish inland, on the banks of the Thames River. However, Lord Dorchester prevailed in his wishes to have the capital established at Toronto, and on July 30, 1793, Lieutenant-Governor Simcoe's wife, Elizabeth, two of their six children, a number of officials and a company of green-coated Queen's Rangers, arrived at Toronto on the schooner, *Mississauga,* to be joined soon after by Lieutenant-Governor Simcoe.

The ship was met and guided into the harbour by Jean Baptiste Rousseau, sometimes called the "first citizen of Toronto". Aside from a few native huts, his was the only building near the site of the new town, where he had lived since the occupation of the area by the French had ended thirty-four years before. During that time he had engaged in trade with the native people and had been involved in arranging the Toronto purchase by the English, of whom he was a strong ally. A Provincial plaque to-day marks the site of his home near the Humber River.

Military strategy was the basis of planning for the new Town, which Lieutenant-Governor Simcoe christened York on August 27, 1793, soon after the welcome arrival of news of the Duke of York's victory in Holland in a skirmish with the French. Thus the name Toronto, which had been applied to the general area since at least 1673, temporarily passed from the scene. The town, which first was little more than a small village, was established in the area fronting on Lake Ontario bounded by present streets, Adelaide, to the north and George and Berkeley to the west and east respectively.

The imposition on the rough terrain of a rigid grid system, later extended throughout the City of Toronto, is probably the most significant of the present-day physical remnants of Simcoe's administration. The town was laid out in the form of ten blocks bordering a shoreline considerably north of the present one, the water coming almost up to what is now Front Street. Simcoe's approach to the naming of streets reflected his loyalty to and affection for the English Royal Family of George III. Thus, the names George, Frederick, (after the Duke of York, the King's son) Princess, (originally Princes, after the five sons of George III), and King, originally applied to Front Street), became permanent Toronto memorials to Royal influence in the Town of York.

The Town of York was close to the site where Simcoe intended that his naval arsenal be built. To protect this operation, a garrison of up to two hundred men was established in a fort far to the west, near what is now the foot of Bathurst Street. It was close to the lake, which then came up to the grounds of what we know as Fort York. The latter fort was laid out and built in the period 1813-16 close to the one which housed the first garrison, near Garrison Creek, one of several water courses which emptied into Lake Ontario between the Humber and Don Rivers.

The town was laid out on elevated ground about 40 yards from the lake. North of the Town, an east-west road was established and named Lot Street, because it formed the southern boundary of 34 newly-created 100-acre Park Lots, each having a width of 20 chains (1,320 feet) and a length of 100 chains (1¼ miles), up to the first concession road to the north. Lot Street later became known as Queen, and the first concession, Bloor. The western-most 32 Park Lots were intended to be suburban estates to be given to officials of the government and others involved in the administration of the new capital. This system resulted in the creation of an instant aristocracy in the new town, and as such, an extension of the English way of life. It also had the effect, in the later period, of delaying expansion of the town to the north.

THE PARK

Important to the development of what would later be known as Cabbagetown, was the fact that the two easterly Park Lots, between the present Parliament Street and the Don River, were to be reserved for government purposes. This decision naturally sprang to Simcoe's military mind as fulfilling a number of objectives. One was to preserve for ship-building purposes the stands of gigantic red and white pine trees which grew on the hills surrounding the Don. These trees, some of them centuries old, reaching a height of 170 feet and having a diameter of 6 feet, were so large that they blocked out the sun from the floorland below, so that almost nothing else grew there. The wind blowing through their top branches created a dull roar, chilling the hearts of early settlers, whose first goal in life was to clear the land for a homestead.

A second purpose achieved by the creation of this government reserve or "Park", was to make land available for intended government buildings and other public institutions. The first government buildings for the Province of Upper Canada were erected during the period 1794-96 on land just east of the present Berkeley Street, south of what is now Front Street. The buildings, one hundred feet apart, were of brick, built as two wings to what was intended to be a larger central Government House. Each measured twenty-four by forty feet. One was to house the Legislative Council, the other the Assembly. The southernmost one also temporarily housed the Court of King's Bench. The two structures were joined by a covered walkway attached at their east ends.

Surrounding these buildings to the north and west, around the banks of Taddle Creek, another of the early watercourses flowing through Toronto to Lake Ontario, were large stands of oak trees, part of the huge forests which originally stood along the lake front between the Don and Garrison Creek and, indeed, throughout the distance of the shore-line of Lake Ontario. The existence of the "Palace of Government" at this site gave rise to the name Palace Street for what is now Front, and to the name Parliament Street, first applied to what is now Berkeley, and later to the more important north-south road which we know by that name to-day.

The "Park", also known as the "Common" remained relatively vacant for many years, delaying settlement until well into the 1840's, by which time parts of it had been granted for hospital purposes, for the laying out of two large cemeteries and a park at its north end, and for gas works and a jail at its south end.

In addition to the Park, the Government also kept for its own purposes the peninsula and the irregular lakefront lands, shown on early maps as "Reserved for the Public as a Promenade" or "Reserved for Public Pleasure Ground". The large lots fronting on the bay were set aside for government officials and prominent citizens, the intention being that they would build substantial two-storey houses, with controlled set-backs and a uniform architectural style. This objective was never fully achieved.

It was anticipated that parts of the Park would be subdivided for future controlled expansion of the town to the east. However, the presence of large marshy swamps around the Don River and Ashbridges Bay, and the feeling that such an environment created unhealthy conditions, contributed to the fact that the Town expanded instead to the west and north. Taddle Creek, which flowed across the north of the Town, cutting off Lot Street near its intersection with the present Sherbourne Street, where it formed a marsh, known as the "Meadow", also acted as a barrier to development of the land northeast of the Town.

ELIZABETH POSTHUMA GWILLIM SIMCOE

One of the most prominent residents of the early Town of York was Elizabeth Simcoe. She was born Elizabeth Gwillim in 1766, months after the death of her father. Her mother, too, died, hours after her birth, thus giving rise to her peculiar middle name. Arriving at York with her husband, in 1793, her keen intelligence and sense of humour made her immediately the popular centre of social life in the growing Town. She spoke French and German fluently, and some Spanish. As an artist, her fine water colour and pen and pencil sketches of the scenes which she saw formed an important and lasting pictorial account of this early period in Canadian history. She kept a daily diary throughout the period from September 7, 1791, nine days prior to her departure for North America, until the Simcoes' return to London in 1796. This diary, together with her artwork, have been preserved, and were published with annotations, by John Ross Robertson, in 1911. The Diary of Mrs. John Graves Simcoe thus became one of the most significant sources of

Silhouette of Elizabeth Posthuma Gwillim Simcoe, 179- , by an unknown artist
— The Baldwin Room, Metropolitan Toronto Library, Ref: T. 13782

historical information about the founding of the Town of York.

On July 30, 1793, she wrote: "We went in a boat two miles to the bottom of the bay and walked thro' a grove of oaks, where the town is intended to be built...The water in the bay is beautifully clear and transparent.[5] On August 11, 1793 she wrote: "This evening we went to see a creek which is to be called the River Don."[6]

Castle Frank

On October 29, 1793, the Simcoes travelled up the Don River to a point north of Winchester Street, where Mrs. Simcoe reports having seen a bald eagle sitting on a blasted pine. They climbed up what was described as a "suger-loafed" hill to the highest spot, overlooking the Don River, on one side, and the brook that flowed through the ravine north-east of the present St. James Cemetery, on the other. The decision was taken to build a house on this picturesque spot, which was included in a lot of two-hundred acres which Lieutenant-Governor Simcoe had taken in the name of his son, Francis. This would be in accordance with the law that required that a house be built on such lands within a year of the grant. It is likely that the Simcoe's name for the cottage, "Castle Frank", referred to the name of their landowner son, who was then four years old.

Work on the cottage commenced in 1794, and the exterior was completed by 1796. Several times Elizabeth Simcoe registers in her diary her displeasure at the slowness of the work. Her bitterness about this fact is quite understandable when it is realized that pending the completion of the work the Simcoes lived in a tent, or "canvas house" previously owned by Captain Cook, the explorer, and purchased second-hand in London by John Simcoe. Mrs. Simcoe had hoped that the site of Castle Frank was high enough to get away from mosquitoes, but on April 2, 1796, she mentions sardonically that "the mosquitoes arrived at three o'clock."

Castle Frank was constructed entirely of white pine. It measured thirty feet across by fifty feet deep and faced south. The trunks of four large sixteen foot high pine trees acted as columns supporting a pediment in what Mrs. Simcoe described as "the plan of a Grecian temple". There were no windows on the north or south sides. The four windows on the east and west sides were never glazed, but were equipped with heavy shutters. The pine log walls were clapboarded, but the interior was never finished.

The Simcoes spent many happy days at Castle Frank, and regularly entertained guests there, especially during the early summer of 1796. The soldiers of the Garrison cut and graded a narrow carriageway and bridle path from the town through shady pine plains covered with ferns. The north-south part of this trail followed the route of what was later known as Parliament Street. It appears likely that the carriages of the Simcoes and their guests turned off this route somewhere in the vicinity of the present St. James Cemetery, although Dr. Scadding suggests that the trail may have followed the path of Winchester Street. Often the Simcoes would travel to Castle Frank by boat up the Don, or, in the winter, by sleigh.

July 20, 1796 was the last day at Castle Frank for the Simcoes. After their departure from York the cabin was used sporadically by Administrator Peter Russell, but it was not used after 1807. In 1829 it burned down, the victim of a fire accidentally set by fishermen.

INVASION OF THE TOWN OF YORK

The Town of York was captured twice by the Americans during the War of 1812. Lieutenant-Governor Simcoe's optimism about the defensibility of the Toronto harbour assumed some degree of naval control of the Lake around it, which was not the case when the American fleet of thirteen ships was first seen south of Gibraltar Point. The town was ill-prepared to defend against the invaders, who landed about one and a half miles west of the garrison and pressed the attack on foot. The chief aggressive action launched by the defenders was the possibly-accidental blowing up of their own powder magazine, which killed the American General Zebulon Pike and many of his soldiers, together with some of the troops of the garrison.

The Americans stayed for five days, during which time the Parliament Buildings and other public buildings were burned down, many stores were looted and a number of prisoners freed. A government ship, the *Sir Isaac Brock,* in the process of construction, was destroyed by the British troops to prevent it from falling into the hands of the Americans.

Later in the same year, on July 31, an American fleet of twelve ships entered Toronto harbour and landed several boat-loads of troops. Once again, some prisoners were liberated and stores looted, and an expedition of three ships was sent up the Don River in an unsuccessful search for ammunition and valuables which had been hidden there by some young men of the Town, including Ely and George Playter. There is some reason to believe that the Americans may have seen maps showing the location of Castle Frank and decided to plunder this "castle" of its no-doubt untold wealth. If such is the case they must have been sadly disappointed to find nothing but a deserted falling-down old cabin designed like a Grecian temple. The second "occupation" lasted less than a day.

The capture of York seems to have had little lasting effect on either the progress of the war or on the town itself. The town did lose a piece of fire apparatus, and the Province lost its Mace, the Royal Standard of George III, and a ceremonial wig from the Speaker's chair, which the Americans apparently took to be part of a human scalp. All of these items were carried off to Washington. It is said that the British burning of the Capitol buildings there in 1814 was done in retaliation for the burning of the Government Buildings of York. The American whitewashing of their most important building after that attack led to its being called since that time the "White House". In 1934, during Toronto's centennial celebrations, at the personal command of President Franklin D. Roosevelt the captured Mace of Upper Canada was returned with great ceremony, to the City of Toronto.

THE TOWN BECOMES A CITY

As already mentioned, the Town of York expanded westward, with the present King Street becoming its principal street. Important buildings and institutions, such as the Anglican Church, the market, and a school were built west of the old town. A map of York in 1813 shows that settlement northward and westward had reached to Duchess Street (now Richmond) and New Street (now Jarvis). By 1820, York had a population of 1,240.

Not everyone who visited the Town of York shared Lieutenant-Governor Simcoe's enthusiasm for its location. In 1825, Edward Allen Talbot had this to say:

> The situation of the town is very unhealthy; for it stands on a piece of low marshy land, which is better calculated for a frog-pond or beaver-meadow, than for the residence of human beings. The inhabitants are on this account much subject, particularly in spring and autumn, to agues and intermittent fevers; and probably five-sevenths of the people are annually afflicted with these complaints. He who first fixed upon this spot as the site of the capital of Upper Canada, whatever predilection he may have had for the roaring of frog and for the effluvia arising from stagnated waters and putrid vegetables, can certainly have had no great regard for preserving the lives of his Majesty's subjects.[7]

Anna Jamieson, traveller, writer and artist, also managed to conceal her delight with the amenity of the fledgling capital in winter. In 1836 she wrote:

> A little ill-built town, on low land at the bottom of a frozen bay, with one very ugly church without tower or steeple, some government offices built of staring red brick in the most tasteless, vulgar style imaginable; three feet of snow all around and the grey sullen wintry lake, and the dark gloom of the pine forest bounding the prospect.[8]

The fact that the "town" had been incorporated as the City of Toronto two years previous, makes her remarks that much more scathing. It is a matter of speculation whether her attitude toward Toronto was in any way coloured by the fact that when she arrived here there was no one to meet her, her foot sank ankle-deep in mud, no conveyance was available, and she had to walk a considerable distance through muddy and uninviting streets.

The Act incorporating the City of Toronto was proclaimed in force on March 6, 1834. The boundaries of the City proper were Bathurst Street on the west, a short distance above Dundas Street on the north, Parliament Street on the east, and Lake Ontario on the south. The city was divided into five wards. That part of the city east of Yonge was called St. David's Ward north of King, and St. Lawrence's Ward south of it. The land between Parliament and the Don, and all of the area north of the city to Bloor Street became part of the "Liberties" to their respective adjoining wards. It was intended that the Liberties would act as a rural-urban fringe, with few public services and a low tax rate, which would be added to the wards when population and size of tax assessment warranted it. By 1859, the Liberties had been absorbed into the city.

With the incorporation of the city, the word "York", which had never achieved local popularity in any event, became a thing of the past. To-day, apart from the street grid-pattern, the only landmarks remaining which existed in the original town, are the Bank of Upper Canada (1827) at the corner of Adelaide and George Streets, and the Fourth Post Office (1833) just to the east of it.

THE DON RIVER—A PERVASIVE INFLUENCE

Of great significance to the early development of the City of Toronto, but of particular and lasting importance to the people of Cabbagetown, is the Don River. Mapped in 1688, the Don formed part of a trade route from the St. Lawrence River to the Holland River. When Simcoe arrived at Toronto the Don was a fresh, clear, meandering stream, teeming with salmon and many other fresh-water fish. Many early writers have recorded seeing Indians fishing for or spearing salmon in the Don. The last recorded catching of a salmon in the Don occurred in 1874.

The Don soon assumed importance as a transportation route to the many mills and other business concerns established on it north of the Town. These included Parshall Terry's saw and grist mills, (later operated by John Eastwood and Colin Skinner, who also had paper mills); the Helliwell brewery; York paper mills; and Eastwood's distillery.

In those early days, the lower Don Valley was covered with mixed deciduous and coniferous forests, and was the home of wolves, deer, black bear, elk, wolverine, marten, porcupine, lynx, bobcat and muskrats. Large flights of migratory birds and passenger pigeons flew overhead, and huge coveys of waterfowl nested in the large marshes which surrounded the Don in its lower reaches and around its mouth. At that time, long before the Don was straightened, it wound lazily down its valley, turning slightly to the east before entering the Lake through two channels, known as the 'Great Don' and the 'Little Don'.

The Great Don was about sixty feet across at the mouth. In 1806, a floating bridge was erected across it for horses and pedestrians. In 1822 new bridges were built across both of the Dons. Upstream, the first bridge across the Don was nothing more than a fallen butternut tree near Winchester Street, known as "Playter's Bridge". In the same year as that "bridge" was in use, (1794), a second bridge called "Scadding's Bridge", was constructed at the present Queen Street, which linked York to the Kingston Road, upon its completion by Asa Danforth in 1800.

Many of the early bridges, (and some later ones too), were washed out by the frequent spring ice jams and flooding which have recurred on the Don through much of its history. In 1813, the bridge at Queen Street was deliberately burned by British troops led by General Sheaffe, as they retreated eastward out of the Town during its invasion by the Americans. Needless to say, the townspeople were not overly impressed with the level of protection afforded to them at that time, and General Sheaffe was bitterly criticized by John Strachan and others who had to deal with the unwelcome visitors.

In 1837, a later Don bridge at Queen, a covered one, was also set afire, this time by a group of William Lyon Mackenzie's rebels, led by Capt. Peter Matthews, who had been detailed by Mackenzie to burn the bridge, intercept the mail, and create a diversion for the militia, to allow the main body of rebels to move down Yonge Street from Montgomery's tavern. However, unknown to the rebels, the volunteer crew of the *British America,* a new fire engine of a type known as a "fore and aft", was patrolling the streets on guard against both fires and rebels. Upon receiving the report of a fire at the Don bridge, the crew rushed to the scene, trundling with them the *British America.* At the sound of the rumbling of the engine's heavy wheels and thinking that artillery was being brought to bear, the rebels disappeared, leaving the crew of the *British America* to put out the fire and save the bridge.

The existence of the Don River and its valley has played an important role in the development of this area and in the history of Cabbagetown. One obvious effect has been the barrier it has posed to eastward expansion of Toronto, particularly in view of the precarious nature of the bridges during the Don's frequent floods before its "improvements" in the 1880's, about which more will be said later. In fact, it was not until the building of the Prince Edward Viaduct, in the period 1915-18, that the area east of the Don north

A group of Cabbagetown boys returning from the Don Valley after a fishing expedition. The fishing rods are cut sticks. The hooks are probably bent pins. But at least there were fish in the Don to be caught.
—City of Toronto Archives: Salmon 1193

"The Artist's Choice, on the Don River", probably a photograph of well-known local painter and commercial artist, Owen Staples, c. 1905
—*From a Postcard*

of Gerrard Street was developed.

As well as a physical barrier, the Don River also posed an impediment to progress because of what was considered its unhealthy environment. The high pine trees which originally stood on the banks of the Don, by retaining moisture, provided breeding grounds for mosquitoes, as did the swampy marshes that surrounded the river near its opening to the lake. Although the connection between mosquitoes and the malaria fever which they spread had not yet been established, nevertheless a popular feeling developed that the marshes of the Don River and Ashbridge's Bay were the source of fever and ague. This attitude that the east end of the city was an unhealthy place, together with other factors, retarded the development of the area later known as Cabbagetown. This prejudice against the east end also, no doubt, affected the attitude that residents of other parts of the city felt toward the impoverished immigrants who first settled this area after the 1840's.

The presence of the Don as a source of water and as a transportation route also led to the concentration of industry around it, particularly mills, distilleries, breweries, tanning and meat packing companies, and iron and gas works. This in turn made the area that much less desirable for those who didn't have to work at the factories, and provided land for the many small boxy labourers' dwellings that grew up around their places of employment. Thus, as the "respectable" centre of the city moved west, the former Park and future Cabbagetown began to receive its new residents.

Another part that the Don has played in the life of Cabbagetown is in providing a place for recreation, which will be described later. However, one fact that will be noted at this time is the role that the Don played in the literary and artistic life of the community. Many of Toronto's most accomplished writers and authors strolled through the Don, using the river and its abundance of wild life, flora and picturesque scenes as the subject-matter of their work. Elizabeth Simcoe sketched here, as did, in later years, Paul Kane, who as a boy spent much of his time here talking to Indians. Henry Scadding, from his earliest days, would sit on the banks of the Don and describe the scenes which he saw there, as did Anna Jameson. Ernest Thompson Seton used his observations of wildlife in the Don Valley for his books *Two Little Savages* and *Wild Animals I Have Known*. Fred Brigden, C.W. Jeffreys and Owen Staples, all excellent and well-known artists who lived in the area, enjoyed portraying scenes of the Don. In more recent times the Don Valley has been the haunt of conservationist Charles Sauriol, whose book *Remembering the Don*, has just been published.

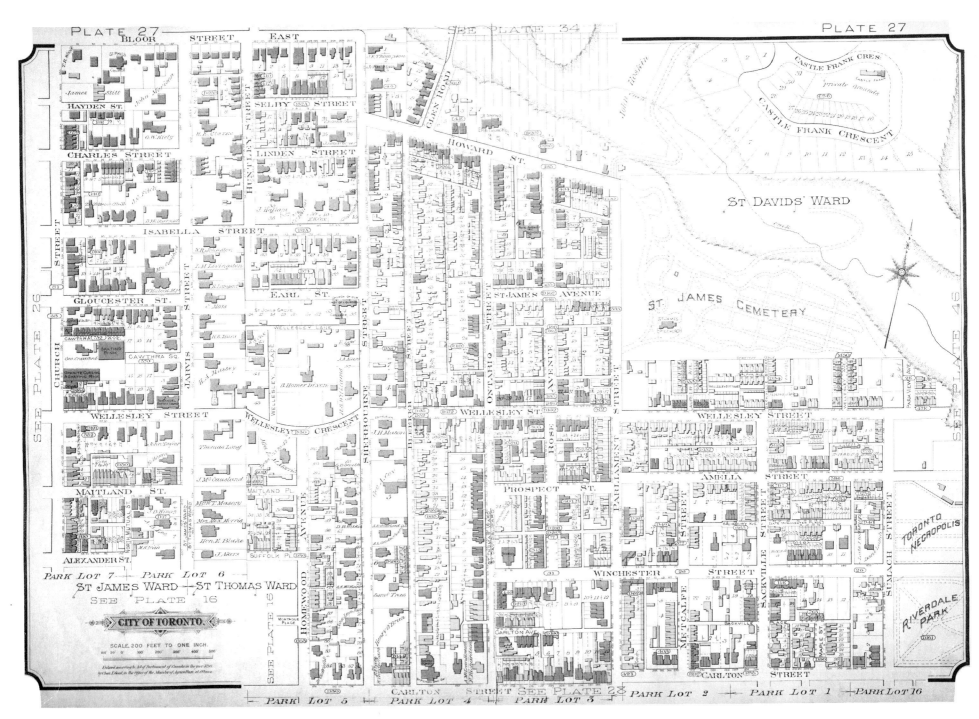

Street maps from an insurance atlas published by Chas. E. Goad in 1890.

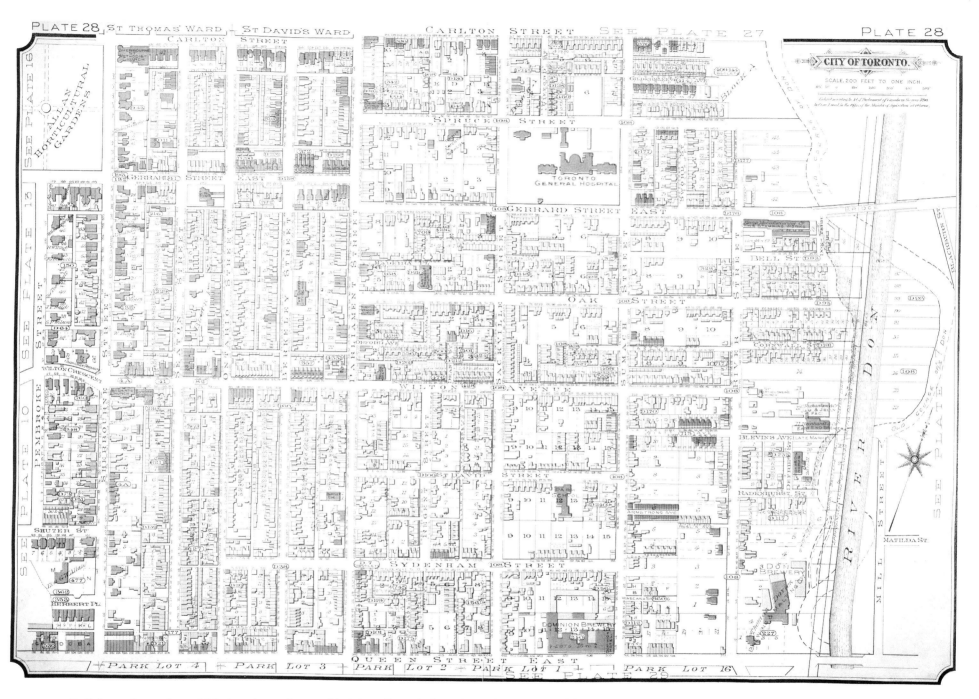

Buildings shown in red (dark coloured) are of brick Yellow (light coloured) ones are of frame construction

PLATE 29
PLATE 29

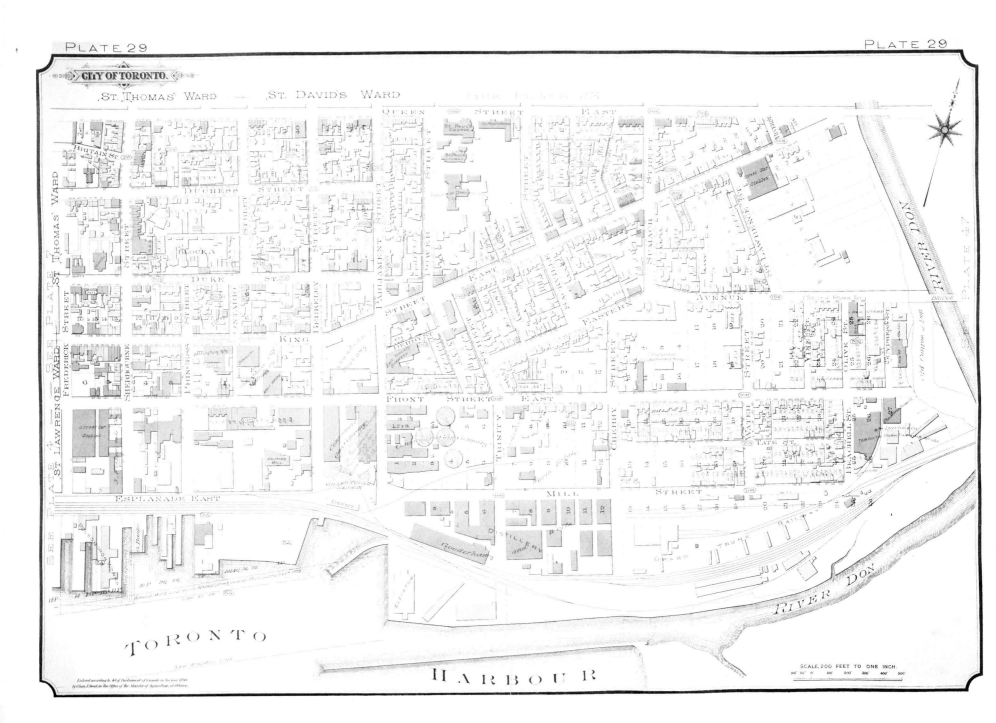

THE SETTLEMENT OF CABBAGETOWN

It didn't happen overnight. An 1842 map of Toronto shows extremely sparse settlement east of Berkeley Street. The only institutional buildings depicted were a jail, (built in 1840 on the site of the old Government Buildings, which were rebuilt in 1820 after their destruction in 1813, but themselves burned down in 1824); the first St. Paul's Roman Catholic Church, on Power Street, (built in 1826, at that time the Cathedral church of the Diocese of Kingston); and the Gooderham and Worts windmill, (built in 1832). A small gas works building (erected in 1841), is shown at the foot of Princes Street (later known as "Princess"). A map drawn in 1851 shows little change from this situation, except that by then two large cemeteries, St. James and Necropolis, had been laid out at the north end of the former Park.

By 1862, when the next map of the City was published, extensive subdivision of land into very small lots in the south end of the Park, particularly around some major industries established there by that time, indicates that settlement had begun in earnest. This is not to say, however, that the area later known as Cabbagetown was heavily populated, for there was still little in the way of development north of King Street. The major buildings shown on this 1862 map are the large gas works complex south of Palace (Front Street) between Parliament and Trinity, (1855); the Grand Trunk Railway workshops and C.S. Gzowski Rolling Mills (beside the sole Railway line into the City, opened in 1856); St. Paul's Church, and the House of Providence, (1857) to the south of it; Trinity Church, (1843); and the Enoch Turner Schoolhouse, (1848) south of it on Trinity Street; public schools, Cherry Street (1859) and Park, (1853), the latter on St. James Street, later St. David Street; and the Toronto General Hospital, (1856) on the north side of Gerrard, between Pine (now Sackville), and Sumach. The history of these institutions will be described later in the book.

Between 1841 and 1861, the population of Toronto tripled, from 14,249 to 45,288. Much of this increase resulted directly from the severe potato famine which devastated Ireland in the 1840's. This catastrophe, together with its accompanying epidemic of fever and cholera, and the hard-heartedness of many Irish landlords, forced the massive emigration to North America of shiploads of the aged and infirm, helpless widows with large families, and others enfeebled by sickness and destitution. Strict immigration policies in the United States closed the door to these "Fever Fleets", resulting in one hundred thousand of these unfortunate people claiming Canada as their new home during the first six months of 1847.

Many settled in the east end of Toronto, with substantial numbers of those of the Roman Catholic faith establishing themselves in shacks and small cottages around St. Paul's Church south of Queen and east of Parliament Street, while those who were members of the United Church of England and Ireland settled in similar accommodation in other parts of the same area. Partly due to tradition, but mainly out of necessity, many of these new Canadians, particularly the Irish, began to grow gardens in the small lots around their homes. The prominent vegetable in these gardens was the cabbage, for which the sandy soil and climate provided ideal growing conditions. In time, the presence of these large leafy vegetables in so many of the Irish immigrants' lots gave rise to the term "Cabbage Town", being applied to the area by non-Irish Torontonians. However, as neighbourhoods developed and hard-won survival realized, what began as a term of derision, later became a source of pride.

Not all of them survived, however, for sickness travelled with them to the new land. Serious epidemics were no stranger to Toronto, with the worst being the cholera plagues which struck in 1832, 1834 and 1849. To compound the problem, the Irish immigration, on uncomfortable and rat-infested ships, led to a typhus epidemic striking Cabbagetown in 1847, leading to the death of 863 people, among them Bishop Power, who died while ministering to the needs of a dying woman. The Pieta in front of St. Paul's Church, at the corner of Queen and Power Streets, is a memorial to Bishop Power, "who laid down his life for the fever stricken members of his flock" and to the immigrants who died in 1847, and were buried in adjacent ground. Rev. William Honeywood Ripley, the first incumbent of Trinity Church, who served without pay for six years, also succumbed to disease in 1849 as a result of his devotion to this work.

A large number of immigrants from England and Scotland, many of whom were as impoverished as their Irish neighbours, also came to live in this area. However, the Irish influence, particularly that of the Northern Irish, stamped an indelible mark on the character of Cabbagetown, and the heavy early concentration of Irish settlers in the blocks around Queen Street west of the Don must be considered among the most significant factors in any attempt to answer the question, "Where is Cabbagetown?"

Not a great deal has been written about the subsequent development of Cabbagetown, and virtually nothing before the end of the last century. Maps and city directories do, however, show how the former Park filled in with houses during the period 1860-90. Generally, the whole of the area east of Sherbourne to the Don was built upon during this period, and, with the exception of the large swaths of houses destroyed for the building of Regent Park, St.

Toronto in 1834 looking west from the Gooderham Windmill, —Metropolitan Toronto Library, Baldwin Room, John Ross Robertson Collection

Jamestown, and the interchanges for the Don Valley Parkway, a substantial number of these homes remain.

Aside from the large houses on Sherbourne Street, residential development throughout this area was, with one exception, somewhat similar in form. This is not to say that the houses were all the same—anything but. However most of the streets displayed similar mixtures of builder-designed Victorian residential styles, including labourers' cottages, terraces, (attached rows) of 2½ storey front-gabled "gingerbreaded" homes, and a sprinkling of earlier Georgian and later Romanesque house forms.

The one exception to the general homogeneity of streetscapes in the area under discussion, and of significance in discovering the character of Cabbagetown, is the former existence in the lower part of the area of numerous narrow cul-de-sacs and other small streets bounded on both sides by long attached rows of 1½ and 2 storey working-class dwellings. Not all of them were built south of Gerrard Street. Flagler Street and Alpha Avenue, in Don Vale, demonstrate that such "workers rows" were not exclusive to the more southerly parts of the area. However there were far more of them there, narrow, cheaply built, entirely functional buildings, which provided a home to so many Cabbagetowners. Few of them have survived, but a walk down Percy Street or Ashby Place today will impart something of the flavour which characterized the true Cabbagetown.

It appears that the first reference to "Cabbage Town" in popular histories of Toronto occurs in the first volume of *Robertson's Landmarks of Toronto,* published in 1894. Even then, the subject is raised not for the purpose of historical depiction but simply as part of an article on social life in 1796. The passage reads:

> ...no order carriages for 1:30, but walk home with your partners in the grey dawn of the morn, through the rain, through the snow, through the clear, cold frost; perhaps no sidewalk, certainly no street cars or cabs; over the Don or the far end of "Cabbage Town.[9]

It is to be noted that early writers, and many of the "old-timers" writing to-day split "Cabbagetown" into two words, no doubt the proper original name. However, the author will stick with modern usage.

THE PEOPLE OF CABBAGETOWN

Some of what follows is based on interviews recently conducted with old-time residents of Cabbagetown. Thus, its accuracy is dependent on memories of events which occurred between forty and eighty-five years ago. It is clear, however, that the strength of these impressions on the youth of that day, and the all-encompassing influence which living in Cabbagetown had over its children, warrant that in the recollections of these men and woman lie many of the answers to the question "Where is Cabbagetown?"

CABBAGETOWN WAS FOR KIDS

What was it like to grow up in Cabbagetown? A graphic portrayal of Cabbagetown childhood in the period around the First World War is contained in the folowing description of one small incident in the life of Wilfred Parkin, told in his own words:

> When I was a little boy I went to Sunday school. Yes, a long time ago I was a little boy too. I had a very nice Sunday School teacher. One day she said I would like you to come to my house because I am going to have a Christmas party for my Sunday school class. Now she lived on Leuty Avenue which you know isn't far from our church, but I lived far away in Cabbagetown where I was born...the other side of the Don River.
>
> It was winter and it was snowing. I didn't have any carfare so I walked and walked and finally arrived at my teacher's house. We didn't have rubber boots or snow boots then either. My teacher said come in and sit down. It was nice and warm in there. The other children were there too.
>
> She had a nice big cat, and it came right over to me and jumped up my legs, then on my shoulder and began licking my hair and then my neck then it jumped down and started to lick my boots. Well the teacher and other children were very surprised to see the cat acting like that. The teacher said my goodness my cat must like you. I never saw him do that before.
>
> I was very embarrassed because I knew why the cat was doing that. In our house when we had a goose for

The boys' game room at the Moss Park Recreation Centre, 1916. —*City of Toronto Archives, D.P.W. 52-657.*

Swimming at 'Sandy Banks' almost in the shadow of the Prince Edward Viaduct, which can be seen to the top left, c. 1909. This was actually a swimming class, organized by the city. Some of the boys are wearing belts, so that they could be held up by instructors while learning to swim.

—City of Toronto Archives: James Collection 7339

25

dinner my mother saved the grease from it. When you were sick with a cold it was rubbed in your chest. It was used to waterproof your shoes, then put on your hair to keep it neat, and that is why the cat was licking me. The others never knew, but now you do.

In those days, everyone who lived in Cabbagetown was poor. There were no cars or television sets, and no planned playgrounds. Kids played on the streets, the vacant lots and back lanes, and on the Don flats. The presence of many lanes and small streets, the abundance of trees, and the relative absence of traffic, made the Cabbagetown neighbourhoods a great place to play. There were few organized activities for children so they had to make their own fun. This might involve jumping on the backs of delivery wagons and trucks, or chasing the ice man for ice chips from his truck. Or it might mean the playing of games, such as kick the bottle; piggy-back, (how many people could you hold?); competitions to put a ball into a cap from the other side of the street; sticks and rocks, or hitting sticks; duck on the rock; peelers and robbers; fire (pretending to be firemen); sheep-guard-off; and the old stand-bys—tag, catch, prisoner's base, and follow the leader. Girls skipped Singles, Double Dutch or Salt, Vinegar, Pepper. These games might be played in the schoolyards or on the streets, perhaps with parents watching from verandahs or front steps, and enjoying the presence of their children, around whom their lives revolved.

Going further afield, children loved to play on the Don flats or in other parts of the Don Valley, for, as previously mentioned, the Don played an important part in the Cabbagetown way of life. Riverdale Park, particularly, was an integral part of the old district. The scene of many family picnics, it also provided, as it does now, ice "cushions" in winter and baseball diamonds in summer. Hockey was played with makeshift equipment; anything that looked like a hockey stick would do, and the puck might just as easily be a ball, a chip of wood, or a "road apple", the frozen offering by a horse on a cold winter's day. Knee pads were fashioned from old newspapers. Skates, if they had them, were simply blades costing seventy-five cents if bought on sale at Eaton's, screwed on to one's shoes. Similarly, skis were often nothing more than slats from old barrels, tied on to one's shoes.

In the summer, kids went barefoot. They came to the Don Valley to hike, hold paper chases, play hare and hounds, see the birds and animals at the old Riverdale Zoo, or collect newts, pollywogs or small frogs, to be brought home and shown to parents.

The most popular summer activity for boys was "skinny-dipping" in the Don, at one of at least eight swimming holes. The favourite of these, known as Sandy Banks, Sandy Point, the Ford or

Children playing on the street in Cabbagetown
—Regent Park—A study in slum clearance, by Albert Rose 1958 U of T Press

the High Banks, was situated almost directly under the Prince Edward Viaduct, at the foot of the sugar loaf hill (formerly the site of Castle Frank), which the boys of Cabbagetown even until recently referred to as Sandy Hill. Here on a hot summer afternoon they would gather to enjoy the fast current of the Don over its clean gravelly bottom. The fact that they considered bathing suits quite unnecessary did not, according to Gordon Sinclair, show any lack of modesty, for whenever a train steamed by down the Don Valley the boys would cover themselves with their hands or kneel down in

Winter activities on the "Don Flats" of Riverdale Park, 1914. —*City of Toronto Archives, Parks Dept. 248*

the water. The water in this area was somewhat cloudy, but further upstream, at Todmorden, one could see bottom, even in the deep holes. Another popular activity was to play in the water from fire hydrants when the fire department opened them up for the children during the hottest days of summer.

There were some organized activities for children, particularly if you belonged to the Boy Scouts, which most boys did. The Scouts of All Saints' Church, of which Bill Hambly was a member, went for summer hikes to a wilderness camp up the Don Valley, a half-day's trek from the corner of Wilton (now Dundas) and Sherbourne. Brigdens Printers, a local firm, supplied the Scouts with a trek cart, which they would take up Parliament Street, along Winchester and down into the Don Valley, crossing the Don by the Winchester bridge, which at that time was the furthest north of the Toronto bridges over the Don. The path then wound up the "half-mile hill" of Royal Road to Danforth, which they crossed, ending up eventually at the weir on the Don River near Pottery Road where they camped in tents left over from the Boer War. Brigdens also outfitted the Scouts with the equipment for a band; Bill Hambly says: "It was my great joy to be patrol leader of the Beaver Patrol and beat a drum. I think that was one of the biggest kicks I ever had of being a kid."[10]

Many Cabbagetown children attended summer camps such as the one run by the Star Fresh Air Fund at Bolton, or the one at Jackson's Point operated by the Salvation Army.

Boys also played lacrosse in the Don Valley and football and soccer, often using real pig's bladders. These were obtained by going down to Davies' Packing House near the mouth of the Don and making faces at the workers until they began to pitch bladders and livers at the mischievous boys.

Fishing was also a popular pastime. Almost anytime a boy could go down to the Don and come back with a string of catfish. In the spring, during the sucker run, these fish could easily be netted in the hundreds. To-day it seems that the only fish that can live in the Don is the large, but unloved, carp.

Next to Christmas, the big event of the year was the Sunday School picnic. For some of the churches in more well-to-do neighbourhoods, this might involve a trip across the Lake on one of the steamers, such as the *Corona*, the *Chicora*, the *Chippewa*, or the *Cayuga*. For Cabbagetown children, it more likely meant a ride on the ferries *Bluebell*, *Primrose*, *Mayflower*, or *Trillium* to the Toronto Island, or a trip to High Park. These places were also popular for family picnics. Bill Hambly remembers that his father would fish for pike at Centre Island, and often returned from picnics with enough to feed their family, and those of several neighbours, for a few days. The Hamblys were also fortunate enough to have a summer cottage,

not at Muskoka or Georgian Bay, but at the Toronto Beach, to which they travelled by street car.

The children loved special days, when exciting activities would be provided for them. The twenty-fourth of May was a long-remembered occasion, for it was then that the winter flannels could finally be shed, and stone crackers, squibs and other fire crackers could be obtained. In the morning the boys would march as cadets down University Avenue, shouldering heavy Enfield rifles, some of them remnants of the Crimean War. Some of the younger boys would simply carry sticks more-or-less the size of rifles. Some of the luckier ones got to play in the famous cadet band from Dufferin School, forty drums and one hundred bugles strong. Meanwhile, the girls would decorate monuments in commemoration of the Queen's birthday. In the evening, a mock military battle would be staged at Riverdale Park, with red-coated militia regiments trying to create as much noise and smoke as possible, to the delight of their audience. Similar exercises were conducted on Thanksgiving Day. If it was not windy, the cloud of smoke put up by these battles might remain for several days.

On Halloween, Cabbagetown youths would set garbage barrels on fire in the middle of the street, or watch medical students at the Toronto General Hospital on Gerrard Street lift one of the small "bouncer" street cars off the tracks and leave it there until they felt like putting it back on.

During the summer teen-agers would venture further afield, swimming in the lake at Cherry Beach, or diving off the concrete piers around the ship turning basin and ship canal, or off wooden pilings into Toronto Bay. Or they would gather in the Don Valley for weiner or corn roasts, or other opportunities to fraternalize with those of the opposite sex. Hugh Garner comments in his autobiography about the many times when he would come home from a date with grass stains on the knees of his pants.

The Toronto Street Railway offered free street car rides for young people to go to the popular swimming spots. Many Cabbagetown children, and those from Riverdale and Moss Park, would catch the car which ran from Woodbine along Queen, then King, making their way first to the fruit and vegetable market situated on the site of the present O'Keefe Centre. The long slow ride would be punctuated by singing, and the taunting of passing policemen with "brass button bluecoat, couldn't catch a nanny-goat." Stopping to grab some potatoes or fruit, if they could get away with it, they would walk across the train tracks to the ferry docks to catch the free ferry *Louella*, to Hanlan's Point. There, at what was called "bare-assed beach", later the site of the Island Airport, they would take off their clothes and spend the day swimming, and gathering driftwood and brush for a fire, where the potatoes would be roasted, and fun would be had by all. Another popular leisure spot was Scarborough Beach Park, at the Toronto Beach, where people could enjoy the bike races, water chute, ferris wheel and shooting gallery. Kids also, of course, went to movies, especially nickel matinees on Saturdays, where they would follow the cliff-hanger serials from week to week.

On Sunday night, young men would take their girlfriends to church, followed by a ride on the streetcar Belt Line, which ran on Sherbourne, Bloor, Spadina and King, (tickets: eleven for twenty-five cents on Sundays; six or eight for twenty-five cents other days), before stopping at one of the many excellent ice cream parlours along the way for a David Harum or banana split.

In winter, whole families would go skating on the frozen Don, or tobogganing or bob-sledding on the high hills on the east side of Riverdale Park. The bob-sled runs were laid out with lamp standards between them, the earlier ones having sputtering blue carbon arc lamps, later to be replaced by electric bulbs. Some of the runs were said to be a half mile long, and were very icy. Long line-ups of racing crews would form at the top, waiting with their sleds, some of them twenty-four feet long, brightly coloured, and having steel runners and padded cushions for the crew. Sometimes, on a cold night, a good crew might reach speeds of up to sixty miles per hour. Nearby were two runs for the slower toboggans. From time to time a bobsled or a toboggan, (which was harder to steer), would fly off the run or hit a lamp standard, causing injuries to the crew, but this did not detract in any way from the popularity of the sport. Unfortunately there always seemed to be more people eager to get on the sled at the top than were later available at the end of the run to pull it back up the hill.

Children saved up all summer, accumulating perhaps up to fifty cents, to have a good time at the Canadian National Exhibition. Tickets were distributed free to schoolchildren, who would spend the whole day there. Many attended the Grandstand show, which cost five cents. In those days the entertainment consisted of a military pageant, illustrating such epic battles as the siege of Lucknow or the Battle of Queenston Heights. At the end of the show a military band played "Rule Britannia", and the kids came home, laden down with maps, pamphlets and souvenirs, having celebrated the end of summer, and looking forward, with little enthusiasm, to a long school year.

In the earliest days of Cabbagetown, the 1840's and 50s, children attended Enoch Turner, Cherry Street, Park, or Parliament Street (at the north-east corner of King) public schools. However, more recent Cabbagetowners attended the new Park School (built 1915-17), on Shuter Street; Dufferin School (built on Berkeley Street, opened in 1877), Cabbagetown's best-known school; Winchester

School (on Prospect Street, 1874); Sackville Street School, (1887); or Rose Avenue Public School, (1884). All of the Victorian buildings which first housed these schools, with the exception of Sackville Street, have been replaced with newer buildings. Throughout this period, children of high school age would attend Jarvis Collegiate Institute or one of the technical schools east of the Don.

The school yards around some of the earlier schools were segregated, with boys in one yard and girls in another. Cabbage-towners who attended Park School in their youth remember that each class would be confined to one class room and would be taught all subjects by the same teacher. Hours attended were from nine o'clock to noon. Grades were numbered with a junior and senior year for each academic period, so that after kindergarten, Grade 1 would be Junior First, and Grade Eight was Senior Fourth.

Marion Lint, who attended Park School, and then went on to Dufferin, comments: "Failures were common, as no one got through unless they knew their school work." She notes that her left-handed brother was made to write with his right hand, causing a speech impediment, stuttering, which took two years to undo.

There were few organized school activities, unless some individual teacher, such as Mr. Richardson or Mr. Ward, at Park School, decided to train students in special fields, in that case soccer, football and running. Rose Avenue School was also known for its athletic programme.

Children marched into school, two-by-two, to the tune of military music. The strap was used quite often on recalcitrant pupils.

In 1908 the Toronto Board of Education instituted a programme of supervised playgrounds in the yards of downtown public schools, "to protect the children" from all kinds of evil, and by seeing that "their language and conduct were at all times of proper character." By 1916 there were seventeen of these playgrounds, one at Sackville Street School.

Marion Lint says that Park School was the toughest school around: "Whenever anyone from another school had to go there for manual training they would wait until two minutes to nine and then run into the class. When they were through for the day the teachers would let them out five minutes before the regular Park kids so they could start running."

St. Martin's School began in a house on Winchester Street, operated by Ursuline nuns. Gloria Rankin recalls that "the nuns kept a bucket of water and soap in the cloakroom for those children who arrived in a less than respectable state".

Wilton Avenue Fire Hall, which stood at the north-east corner of Dundas and Parliament, was just a stone's throw from Dufferin School. When the big bell in its high tower sounded to signal an

Fire reel, No. 7 station, Dundas and Parliament Streets, c. 1895. —A Toronto Album, Glimpses of the City That Was, Mike Filey, 1970.

A senior third (grade six) class at Dufferin School, 1898 —*Dufferin School Old Boys' Association Year Book, 1931*

alarm, the boys playing in the schoolyard would rush to Parliament Street to see the horse-drawn fire reel, (literally, a one-horse two-wheeled wagon holding a large reel of hose), clatter out of the station "with gong clanging, sparks flying, and firemen hanging on by their eyelids while they worked their way into rubber coats and boots".[11] If the call was to Box 247, (Gerrard and River), the boys would stay at the fence to see the four-wheeled reel from Berkeley Street, the hook and ladder from Lombard station, the hose wagon from Yonge Street, and perhaps the reel from Rose Avenue, go flying by. Such a performance provided great thrills to the schoolboys, and great frustration when it occurred during the school hours. More than one boy who because of this excitement couldn't concentrate on his work, was strapped or required to stay late to write "fire" one hundred times on the blackboard while his mates went off to see the fire.

Similar thrills attended watching the police load and unload prisoners into the Black Maria, or paddy wagon, at the Don Jail, or on the street after a "pinch".

Another institution serving Cabbagetown children was the East End Day Nursery, established about 1905 in a large Victorian house at 28 River Street, just north of Queen. When Hugh Garner was taken there by his mother, the cost was ten cents a day. He remembers it particularly for the wagons and sleighs of the New Method Laundry next door, which provided a natural jungle gym for the children. The nursery also took older children before and after school and at lunch time, to enable their parents to complete their ten hours of hard work each day. The East End Day Nursery continued in operation until well into the 1930s. After World War II, the building was torn down and replaced by a Brewers' Retail Store, which, says Hugh Garner, "is a much truer projection of the social

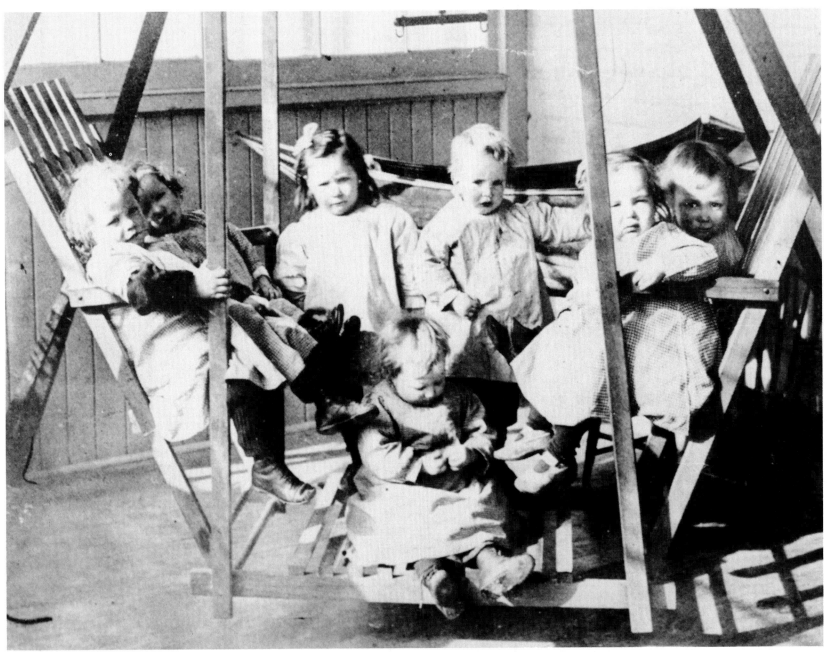

East end day nursery. This photo, used in several of the nursery's annual reports, was entitled "Having a Good Time", hardly descriptive of the children's faces.

—Baldwin Room, Metropolitan Toronto Library Ref. No. T11851

East End Day Nursery, c. 1905, with contemporaneous touch-ups. Baldwin Room, Metropolitan Toronto Library Ref. No. T11846

"Children at the side of the coal shed" in Cabbagetown, c. 1912
—Arthur Caine

An unidentified child outside of 19-21 St. Paul Street, A "Labourer's Cottage", c. 1915
—Athur Caine

character of the neighbourhood."

Across River Street from the Day Nursery was the Evangeline Settlement House, a neighbourhood building which, according to Hugh Garner, "contained a preventative medicine clinic, more social workers, and, though I only presume this, classrooms in which baby-care hygiene and crafts were taught". Children would go there to be inoculated against one of the contagious diseases that spread in epidemics across Cabbagetown. They could also obtain small operations there, such as the removal of tonsils. There was no overnight accommodation; after the operation was performed the child would simply be sent home.

Boys were kept in short trousers until they were fourteen or fifteen. The popular outfits were knickers (kneepants) and stockings, surmounted by a shirt or sweater. The day of graduation to long pants, such as flannel "bags", was a momentous one for the young boy, and somewhat embarrassing. Every boy wore a hat or peaked cap. Girls wore blouses, sweaters and skirts, smocked dresses, or jumpers. The school uniform for girls attending Jarvis Collegiate consisted of a white middy, a black tie, navy skirt, long black stockings and white running shoes.

It was only when a uniform was required that Cabbagetown children would look as well dressed as kids from other neighbourhoods. Generally, their clothes, like those of their parents, would be purchased as often as not from one of the charitable clothing depots

or second-hand shoe stores run by the Salvation Army, City Relief office or other similar institution. Similarly, furniture would be obtained from a second-hand furniture store or furniture exchange, of which there was one on Parliament Street.

Almost a uniform for children in Cabbagetown and other poorer areas of the City was the wearing of the leg-length black woollen stockings and itchy puce-coloured woollen sweaters which arrived in the Star Boxes—distributed each Christmas by that newspaper. These packages, about the size of a shoe box, and differentiated for boys and girls, also contained what Hugh Garner describes as a box of over-sweet coloured candies and a small toy. While the recipients would usually sit down to cut a slit in the high roll-down necks of the sweaters to relieve the itchiness, their parents were no doubt genuinely thankful for the newspaper's generosity. Other relief at Christmas came in the form of charity boxes, brought by the Salvation Army, Rotary Club, Kiwanis Club and other similar organizations. Some families put their name on the list for a number of these, rather than only one, as they were supposed to do, thus in some cases guaranteeing a supply of chicken and plum pudding through to the end of January.

Christmas was a family affair, and a week-long festival. Instead of the giving of expensive presents, Cabbagetowners celebrated by dropping in on one another. On Christmas morning they awoke to the peal of bells from Cabbagetown churches such as St. Augustine's, St. Paul's, All Saints', St. Enoch's, Parliament Street Methodist, and St. Simon's.

HOW THEY LIVED

They lived in houses ten to seventeen feet wide, usually attached to others in rows of up to twenty identical units. In some rare cases a house would have been built by the owner, who would first buy the lot, then, when he could afford it, build a house with three or four rooms, and then later would build on to the front or rear of the house. Installing a bathroom would be another major and expensive proposition. Most houses were, however, erected by the professional builders. The buildings were of frame construction, with pine boards fastened to frames, laths nailed on the boards, and the exterior covered with stucco, or roughcast, and the interior walls plastered. There was no insulation, for either heat or sound. There were almost no brick houses, although some of the better frame ones had a brick front, or veneer, affixed to their front walls, and to one side, if it showed.

The typical working-class house had a door to one side of the front wall, with one window or a small three-windowed bay looking out from the parlour at the front of the house. Behind this room was usually another, of approximately equal size, which might serve as the dining room if the family also occupied the upper floor, or a bedroom, if they did not. Behind that room was the kitchen, usually in the "tail" of the house, a part which indented behind the second room, ensuring that every room in the house had a window. In some houses there would be a back parlour between the front parlour and dining room.

On the second floor, two windows looked into the master bedroom at the front, behind which might be a bathroom and one or two smaller bedrooms. The houses tended to be hot in summer and cold in winter. By the 1920s, they were, of course, between thirty and fifty years old, and neglect by landlords or the impecuniosity of the much smaller number of working-class owners, made it unlikely that even a minimum amount of maintenance and repair had been performed. Since the buildings were originally erected in a world without building permits, minimum building standards, or, indeed, any official supervision over builders, many of the workers' cottages were of very poor quality to begin with. Thus, by the end of the First World War, many of them showed their age, with brittle pieces of stucco having fallen off their lath, wide cracks around window and door frames, and various problems with the roof, often resulting in leaks and staining.

By the 1930s, the area was seriously overcrowded, with at least two families living in many houses. Of the houses in Cabbagetown, almost half had no central heating, depending entirely on stoves, one out of ten still had only outside toilets, and about one-quarter

Gilead Place, 1936. A typical street of small houses in Cabbagetown. In 1919, the city directory listed simply "Macedonians" or "Foreigners" for some of the people living in these cottages.
—City of Toronto Archives—D.P.W. 33-62

of them had no bathtub. Many small streets, such as Bright Street, had a row of privies sitting just outside the back doors of the houses.

Hugh Garner describes the sounds and smells of Cabbagetown at the beginning of his novel, *Cabbagetown,* in which the subject of the book, Ken Tilling, returns to his house, (which, the author states in his autobiography, was modelled after homes in which he lived on Wascana Avenue and Blevins Place).

> As Ken hurried south towards his own street he became conscious of the increase in sound. There were more children shouting and crying, more traffic on the narrow streets, more raucous pedlars, and above all this the constant noise of the factories, the whir of machinery, the clang of metal, the increased noise of streetcars on their older roadbeds.
>
> "The smells were also different. Coal smoke, chemicals, horse manure, wet mattresses, old wallpaper and dirty snow. As he passed the open windows of a mill he caught the smell of hot metal curling from the lathes. But the prevailing smell was one of decay, of old wet plaster and rotting wooden steps, the smell of a landlord's carelessness and neglect."[12]

#628 #626 #624 #622

A back view of old houses on Dundas Street in 1951 shows the kind of conditions which befell Cabbagetown families. These homes were built in the 1870's and are typical of those that existed throughout Cabbagetown.

—City of Toronto Archives—Ref. 9.2.3.W Misc. 798

As previously stated, many of the houses in Cabbagetown didn't have central heating. This meant that in the cold months of winter, someone had to make sure that a ready supply of wood or coal was available. Fuel also had to be obtained throughout the year for the stove in the kitchen, used for cooking and, in many cases, heating bath and laundry water. The piping for the other stoves might be dismantled during the warm months, and then re-installed at the onset of cold weather in the Fall.

The children of the family might be made responsible for obtaining wood for the stoves. Resourcefulness turned up the fact that much wood was readily available at the St. Lawrence Market, in the form of discarded fish boxes. Obtaining coal was a bit harder, especially if you didn't have the money to pay for it, (although during the Depression "pogey" coke or coal was available). A source of coke was the Consumers' Gas Works (south of Front Street between Berkeley and Trinity Streets.) After the gas had been extracted from the burning of coal, the ashes would be dumped out. This was a continuous process, as was the work of the Cabbagetown children who would appear on the scene to search through the ashes for coke, which would be taken home for fuel.

Another source of fuel was the Kemp Manufacturing plant (later known as General Steel Wares), which stood at the south-east corner of River and Gerrard Streets, and was one of the area's major employers. Local residents paid nightly visits to Kemp's coal pile to "borrow" some badly needed fuel. A real bonanza might be enjoyed by the pickers if a train car full of coal waiting for unloading, was left unattended for the night. Somehow the police, who no doubt knew of the pilfering and also of the need for it always seemed to be looking in the other direction when it occurred.

Once the fuel was gathered, it had to be kept ready for stoking the fire from time to time. One of the most uncomfortable times remembered by several of the old-timers was coming down in the morning to find the fire out, the pipes full of ice, and one's socks frozen.

Mary McKeown, who lived in one of a row of houses on the south side of Gerrard, near River, reports that although the row did have central heating, one unfortunate by-product was that whenever one of the residents gave the house a good cleaning, it drove the bedbugs and other vermin into the other units, requiring them to have a good cleaning to get the pests to go back. Some people kept cats or terriers to catch mice, and rat traps were often found to be required.

Although electric lighting was available, many homes in Cabbagetown were still lit by gas lamps well into this century. Gas lamps had to be looked after, their wicks trimmed and their mantles replaced from time to time, and they had to be refilled. The state of

The O'Neill public baths, north-west corner of Sackville and St. David Streets. The picture was taken in 1914, two years after the building was erected.   —City of Toronto Archives, Ref. 9.2.3.G 797

the art in matches was a type of long sulphur-headed torch which was quite smelly when lit. One had to be careful not to touch the light-diffusing mantle with the match, since it was extremely fragile and might disintegrate, causing curses all around.

Electric or gas refrigerators were to be found in some homes. However a great number still used the ice-box, into which were placed twenty-five to fifty pound blocks of ice delivered by a man with a truck or wagon, who would carry the ice into the house by means of a pair of large metal tongs.

Although some houses had bathtubs, many did not, so on Saturday night water would be heated and poured into a big round tub in the middle of the kitchen floor. After every family member had bathed, the water would be thrown outside or poured down the toilet. Some families sent their children each week down to the O'Neill public baths, at 188 Sackville Street.

Few Cabbagetown houses had telephones in the early years although they were available. Most of them were black boxes that hung on the wall, although prestigious desk models could be obtained. In 1911, Toronto had five exchanges, North, Main, Adelaide, Junction and Parkdale, the name of which would be followed by a four-digit number.

Cabbagetown Store, John Verner, Prop., 283 Parliament Street

This store is the subject of the book "Cabbagetown Store", by J.V. McAree, 1953 —Baldwin Room, Metropolitan Toronto Library Ref. No. S1-687

Real estate was fairly inexpensive by to-day's standards; a decent five-room home cost less than $2,500., ($400. down) and could be rented for $15. a month. On the other hand, with wages ranging from $10.00 to $20.00 a week, a house was for many a prohibitive proposition. In any event, many residents were content to remain tenants so as to retain mobility. During the Depression years only about one in five Cabbagtowners owned his or her own house.

It was during that period that evictions became more common. Failure to pay the rent could lead to one's furniture and belongings being placed out in the front yard or on the street. A group of residents, led by a man described by Cabbagetown historian, James Ealey, as "a former County Fair fighter from Ireland known throughout the district as "Hammy-the-Mug", formed themselves into an eviction committee, to confront the bailiffs when they tried to evict longtime residents from their homes. At times such confrontations would lead to violence so that police would have to come. In others, the eviction committee simply moved everything back into the house after the bailiffs had left.

FOOD, AND WHERE THEY SHOPPED

At many of the street corners throughout Cabbagetown stood one of the most important insitutions in Cabbagetown life, the corner store. Inevitably such an establishment would be located on the first floor in the front of a small residential-style building. The proprietors and their family would live behind and/or over the store, and all would work in it.

Physically, they seem almost to have been cast from a mould. The large windows in the double bay front would be bounded at the top by strips of advertising supplied to the store by some of the best-known product manufacturers, particularly Salada Tea, Coca-Cola, Pepsi-Cola, Orange Crush, and Black Cat, Winchester and Buckingham cigarettes. In the windows would be displayed, on one side, food, items in cans or boxes neatly stacked to attract the passerby, and on the other, containers of glistening fresh fruit and vegetables.

Once inside, the customers would be treated to the sight of an amazing variety of not only staple food items, but all manner of dry goods, hardware, kitchen utensils, cosmetics, drugs, dishes, articles of clothing and perhaps even shoes. For this was a small general store serving its neighbourhood in every way it could, and no storekeeper wanted to be caught not having exactly what his customer wanted.

The corner store was more than simply a place where people

Corner store, at one time Spiegel's Groceteria, at the south-east corner of Sumach and Oak Streets, shown in 1947.
—City of Toronto Archives Ref: Housing 958

went to buy necessaries. It was a social centre, a place to catch up on local gossip, to ask for advice, to inquire about the state of health of a neighbour or find out whether another neighbour had yet found a job; to complain about the weather or the government; and generally, to feel better by having the opportunity to discuss things with a friendly and sympathetic person. As pointed out by Sophie Spiegel Stransman, whose parents, Max and Naomi Spiegel operated Spiegel's Groceteria, at the south east corner of Sumach and Oak, a store-keeper also functioned as a sort of social director, and at times dietician, practical nurse, music or fashion consultant, and, on occasion, even marriage counsellor.[13]

One of the best-known of the corner stores in Cabbagetown was that of John Verner, at 283 Parliament Street (since demolished), for it was this establishment which was immortalized by J. Verner McAree in his book *Cabbagetown Store*.[14] The book depicts the years of the author's childhood, in which he lived at the store with his Uncle John and Aunt Polly, who ran the business from the 1870s until the end of the First World War. He describes the importance of such a store to the neighbourhood it served, which was a small one because there was such an establishment on almost every block, as well as larger ones, such as Radcliffe's, later Cork's (north east corner of Queen and Parliament), at some of the major intersections.

Carson Stong, his father, G.R. Stong, and a delivery boy stand in front of the "Twin" Stong stores at 252-254 Queen Street East at Seaton Street c. 1910

McAree portrays the way in which the family life of the owners, as well as that of many of their relatives and neighbours, revolved around the store. He describes the long hours that they worked, for one of the advantages which the small store had over its larger competitors was that it would be open quite late, so that a customer might drop over, as the need occurred, to pick up a half pound of butter or a quart of milk.

Another thing that the small store provided for its customers that they could not get elsewhere, was credit. There were few cash sales. Most of the regular customers, who earned wages of perhaps ten dollars a week for ten to twelve hour days, would pay up on Saturday for goods bought during the previous week, "or present plausible reasons for not paying it." Often the store would lend money to one of its customers to tide him over to the end of the week. If he lost his job, he would be penniless within two weeks. This wouldn't, however, mean that he would be cut off from credit, for it was felt that at this time he most needed help, and as long as he could make arrangements for his milk and meat, the store would supply him with whatever else he might require, expecting that when he got back on his feet again he would start paying off his account. Even a customer who had run up a large amount of credit, say fifty dollars, and who satisfied the storekeeper that is was not and never would be within his means to pay it, would not be cut off, but would have his slate wiped clean, in the hope that he would become once again a paying customer.

Although, as was inevitable, this and many other small corner grocery stores finally went out of business because of their own debts, nevertheless, they were an important institution in the life of Cabbagetown, and seem to have typified the spirit of neighbourliness, warmth and caring which gave the area its resilience.

As well as the small corner stores, there were larger ones, such as Radcliffe's, previously mentioned, Greenshields, at north west King and Berkeley; and Cira's at north east Parliament and Carlton. A few of the other Cabbagetown grocery stores remembered by old-timers are: McCormicks, at south east Wellesley and Sackville; Gatto's, on Parliament; Stong's at Queen and Seaton; McNamara's at south east Sackville and Carlton; White's, at north east Parliament and Dundas; Salvatore Badali's fruit market on Parliament, (the first fruit store; previously all fruit was sold at the Market or by push cart); Dove's, at Oak and Parliament; Cummins's at north east Sackville and Oak; and Sammon's on Sackville north of Carlton.

They also remember butcher shops: McMorran's, at Sackville and Amelia, (whose building still has its original wooden canopy out over the sidewalk); Meech's; Silk's; Weston's and Clayton's on Parliament Street; Stong's at Queen and Seaton; Davies' on Queen Street; and Calgie's, at Berkeley and Dundas. Dunlop's Dairy was on Dundas; while Tingle's was on Gerrard, near Sackville. Clark's Dairy was on Ontario Street, and Price's was on Queen, near Sherbourne. Oak Drugs, on Parliament near Carlton, had a lending library. A book could be borrowed for three cents. Hugh Garner remembers paying five cents to rent out *Lady Chatterly's Lover*. Other drug stores remembered by old-timers are Jupp's, on Wellesley Street, and Cruttendens, at Gerrard and Sumach, which after the end of Prohibition became the Avion Hotel, now the Cabbagetown. At the north east corner of Sackville and Amelia was Cranfield's pharmacy, open in that location for over fifty years.

At the north west corner of Carlton and Parliament was Rome's Ice Cream Parlour, remembered by Max Walker as the "classiest ice cream parlour of them all." Mr. Rome, who apparently was of Greek extraction, had the largest stock and variety of candy this side of downtown. He catered to the "carriage trade". Borthwick's Store on Queen Street sold sponge cakes iced in different colours. At Robertson Brothers' Store at Queen and Jarvis, one could buy a whole bag of broken candy for ten cents. At the Christie Brown factory on Adelaide Street, broken cookies could be purchased very cheaply. Another ice cream store was Stuart's, at Sumach and Winchester, which would become, much later, Jeremiah's.

Another of the "carriage trade" stores was Michie's, on King Street downtown, which had many kinds of blended teas with exotic names and in brightly coloured cans. Much of the interior was highlighted by highly polished wood, and coin boxes carrying change whirred overhead. Michies also, before Prohibition, carried a large stock of liquors and wines, as did Greenshield's, which used to sell whisky from a barrel at fifty cents a gallon. In the spring, 'Goat' signs went up to show that Bock beer had arrived. Many Cabbagetowners would nip over to the local tavern, such as the Broadview or the Shamrock, to fill up a flask for less than forty cents.

Prohibition came on March 22, 1916. Several old-timers remember that Haffey's store, a neighbourhood fixture at the corner of Dundas and Berkeley, had to sell all of its alcohol before the deadline. People lined up to buy G & W Whiskey at seventy-five cents a quart, and on the last day, men were seen sitting and drinking right outside the store. During Prohibition, bootleggers flourished. Alf Statham remembers that there used to be one operating in some garages north of Wellesley up near the cemetery fence in the vicinity of the Owl House. He recalls once having seen a strange car pull up while the bootlegger was at his business. Alf tipped him off that there was a reception committee waiting for him down the road. Quietly, the bootlegger unloaded his car and drove off. The police were shocked to find that they had a dry run. A few days later an envelope left at Alf Statham's house contained some cash, about the amount, he figures, that the fine would have been. Prohibition officially ended on June 1, 1927.

Some of the other small business establishments in Cabbagetown now remembered by its long-time residents are: Morton Montgomery's book and magazine store at Queen Street and Trefann, still in operation to-day; Coatsworth's store at Parliament and Dundas, where a buyer's money was put in a container and swung back to a cashier, who swung it back again if there was change; Walkin Shoes, originally on Queen Street and later on Parliament, still in operation to-day; and Nettleship's Hardware, on Parliament Street south of Wellesley, also still going strong. More will be said later about some of these long-time Cabbagetown business concerns.

As well as the shops, much of the food, produce and goods consumed by Cabbagetowners was brought to them by the various horse-drawn wagons, trucks and pedlars carts which were so prevalent in the period before the Second World War. In fact, some of the streets must have been virtually lined with vehicles of various kinds, and, in the winter, sleighs; for each week Cabbagetown homes would be visited by: a butter and egg man; selling "dairy", as opposed to "creamery", butter; a milkman; a baker's man; a man selling Ocean Blend Tea; (a thriving local business whose delivery men first came in horse-drawn surries with a fringe, then in motorized trucks which looked like a surrey with a fringe), a fish man; and an Italian fruit pedlar, whose cart, bearing such items as pink rhubarb, leaf lettuce, radishes and mounds of bananas, was one of the first signs of spring.

There was also an ice-cream man peddling his product from an open horse-drawn wagon, equipped with a serving bar on each side. There was a choice of biscuit covers or a container for the ice cream, since there were few cones in those days. Ice cream cost a penny.

In addition to the above itinerant salesmen, there were also a number of other delivery men who came from time to time, such as the coal man, the coal oil man, delivery wagons from Eaton's (black horses), and Simpson's, (dapple grey horses), almost all of whom were willing to deliver without charge. In addition, men and boys selling wood would yell "wood" in a loud voice up and down the street, and a junk collector, known to neighbourhood children as the "sheeney man" would plod along the streets with his old horse and broken-down wagon. Finally, to add to the traffic and din was a street merchant remembered by Lorne O'Donnell as "Flypaper John". He sold flypaper, a useful commodity in an area with so many horses and stables. In the hot summer months, he would walk the street, chanting:

I catch 'em alive, two for five; All the blue bottles as well as the flies.

In the evening, post wagons collected the mail from the corner boxes, often acting as a signal to the children that it was time for bed.

Each fall, women would go down to the St. Lawrence Market or the market at Front and Yonge to stock up on baskets of fruit and vegetables, particularly pears, peaches, tomatoes, and cucumbers, in order to preserve them for winter use. They also put up Christmas puddings, tub butter, and eggs pickled in isinglass.

The following are examples of some of the prices paid for commodities in Cabbagetown during the 1920's and 1930's:

Food:	—beef: 15¢ to 25¢ a pound;
	  other meat: 6¢ to 12¢ a pound;
	—sugar: 10 pounds for 46¢
	—coffee: 60¢ a pound, or 40¢ for
	  coffee with chicory in it
	—tea: 35¢ per pound;
	—potatoes: 50¢ a bag
	—sugar: 5¢ a pound
	—butter: 37¢ a pound
	—liver was given away free with other
	  meat purchases

Other:	—cigarettes—e.g. Derbies, Athletes,
	  Sweet Caporals, MacDonald's,
	  Blackstrap, Beaver—5 for 10¢
	—a 12-course meal at one of the better
	  restaurants such as McConkey's,
	  Thomas's, the King Edward, or
	  Queen's Hotel, was $1.
	—a good made-to-measure suit could
	  be had for $10.00

Looking west along Amelia Street across Sackville Street, in 1891. The brick pavement has been partly torn up for sewer construction. To the left, at the S.E. corner of the intersection, is the wooden canopy in front of the stores of Thomas Gardiner, Grocer and George McMorran, Butcher, The canopy still stands. Across Amelia Street is the newly-opened drug store of Eugene Lemaitre, later Cranfield's Pharmacy.

—City of Toronto Archives, Ref. C.E. 14, Vol. 3-8e.

Described only as an employee, Toronto General Hospital, 1870's
—Province of Ontario Archives Ref: S17145

WHERE THEY WORKED

Alfred Pittis was an iron monger. The work of preparing the moulds was so dirty that he instructed his daughters that they need not acknowledge one another on the streetcar.

Mary Pattis McKeown

Few of the Cabbagetown old-timers talk very much about where they or others worked, preferring to remember the more enjoyable aspects of life in Cabbagetown. At least until recently, little was written about working conditions, or the plight of the labourer in Toronto factories, in the early part of this century.

Cabbagetown was always predominantly working class. Throughout the period of its history under discussion, the working people of Cabbagetown found themselves at the bottom of the socio-economic ladder. With very few exceptions, they tended to be unskilled or blue collar, with a very small number, usually city or bank employees, in the white collar class. For that reason, and in view of the fact that Cabbagetown had among the smallest houses and the poorest housing conditions in the city, (rivalled only by the Ward, the area around the Old City Hall), few people could afford to leave it. Instead, the majority of them, who were tenants, might move from place to place in Cabbagetown, but rarely could they save up the money to leave. Hugh Garner once said that the best paths out of Cabbagetown were to become a professional athlete, a theatrical personality or an artist.

As the least skilled labourers, Cabbagetowners were the first and hardest hit by the several severe economic depressions which occurred in the middle 1880's, at the end of the first decade of this century, and, of course, during the great Depression of the 1930s. In the Depression, most Cabbagetown men were unemployed. When they were able to find work, they were most likely to be the lowest paid, the most exposed to dangerous conditions in virtually unregulated industries, the most susceptible to seasonal and other lay-offs, the blacklist, and loss of wages caused by sickness or injury, and the least likely to have the protection of unions. Of course, they also worked the longest hours.

In the early days of Cabbagetown, child labour was quite common, with young children being required to work normal working hours of about sixty hours per week for between one-quarter and half the wages that would be paid to a man—e.g. about four dollars per week. Women, too, were exploited in similar fashion. The Factory Act of 1886, which prohibited the employment of boys under twelve and girls under fourteen, not only didn't put an end to

Workers at the Polson Iron Works, a major industry at the foot of Sherbourne Street, undated.
—*City of Toronto Archives Ref. 9.2.3.G 506.*

Employees of the P.R. Lamb Manufactory, c. 1880

Dorothy Lamb

those practices, but increased the proportion of women employed as cheap labour.

Although there were some good employers, working conditions in the factories of others were abominable. Virtually untrained workers were required to work long hours in hot, unventilated factories, near dangerous unguarded machinery, in overcrowded uncomfortable buildings with bad sanitation. Many people worked at more than one job just to be able to survive, and, in the early days, there was no welfare relief, unemployment insurance, mother's allowances or workmen's compensation.

As mentioned earlier, a number of large industries became established in and around the fringes of Cabbagetown, particularly around the Don River and the lakefront. Around them grew up settlements of workers' houses. People tended to live close to their work, and the most common means of getting to work was on foot.

Some of the Cabbagetown industries at which local people worked were the following: the Consumers' Gas Works, Gendron Manufacturing, Firstbrooke Box Company, Kemp Manufacturing, Gerhard Heintzman Piano Company, Smith Brothers Pioneer Carriage and Waggon Works, Roher Bros. Bottle Works, Toronto Street Railways, Lamb Glue and Blacking factory, Sunlight Soap, Morse Soap, Wickett and Craig Tanners, Davies Pork Packing House, Firstbrooke Slaughterhouse, Carhartt Clothing, Freyseng Cork Company, Richardson's Jams and Jellies, Queen City Vinegar, Lytle's Vinegar, the breweries: Dominion, Korrmann, Don, Copland's, Ontario Brewing and Malting, and Reinhardt's; and Gooderham and Worts Distillery.

At the coming of the Depression, with so many men out of work, families would often be supported by the wages of women, who could find jobs as cleaners or in the textile industry, some working at more than one job. Children, too, found small jobs to supplement the family income. During the winter, men carrying shovels would line up at the City yards on Reed Street, near Gerrard and Sackville, hoping to be able to get jobs cleaning snow off the City's major arteries for one dollar per day. Many families in this period subsisted on relief coupons distributed by the City, which could be exchanged for basic foods at the local grocery store.

During the Depression many men left their families to ride the rails in search of work. Some just gave up. A butcher on Gerrard Street near the corner of Sumach hanged himself in his freezer. It has been said that children in Cabbagetown grew up very quickly during the Depression.

Cabbagetowners to-day point with pride to the fact that by working together and looking after each other they managed to survive through this difficult period of their lives.

Smith Brothers, pioneer carriage and waggon works, Est. 1843
S.W. corner Parliament and Adelaide Streets.
The building still stands, but without its advertising lettering, which was cleaned off in 1979. —Toronto Illustrated, 1893

P. Freyseng & Co., Cork and Bottlers' Supplies, S.E. corner of Queen and Sumach Sts., 1897. The building still stands.
—Toronto, Canada, The Book of its Board of Trade, 1897-8

HEALTH CONDITIONS

Sickness struck families hard. From its earliest days, Cabbagetown had a reputation for miserable living conditions, including the prevalence of bad air and water, filth, dirt and refuse. In 1877, it was reported: "Pine Street [now Sackville] is another bad street in the City for cow pens, and in these there is not the slightest attempt at cleanliness. Queen Street east of Parliament is another locale of pig pens and cow sheds".[15] In 1885, it was stated: "The extreme end of this eastern section, of [King Street] is a dreary wilderness, into which no man ever seems to venture except the aborigines, and in which all the refuse of the city seems to accumulate. It has already been hinted that the unsavoury reputation it bears from a sanitary point of view is probably at the bottom of its want of prosperity."[16]

Much of the work of the Toronto Board of Health during the latter part of the century was involved in trying to improve sanitation in Cabbagetown and other poorer areas of the city. The principal problem was the outdoor privy. By 1912 only two thousand of the fifteen thousand of them remaining in Toronto at the turn of the century, had been removed. Many of these were in Cabbagetown. During that period the City still did not have an adequate system of water supply or sewage disposal. Until 1911, the city dumped its untreated sewage directly into the Toronto bay, not too far from its main water intake.

Toronto was swept by an epidemic of typhoid and diptheria in 1891. Diptheria struck again in 1929-30, and in the mid-1930's there was an outbreak of polio. In the first decade of this century, one out of three babies failed to live to its first birthday.

Ways of dealing with disease were slow in coming, but did come. Inoculations against childhood diseases were made available at the Evangeline Settlement and other medical centres. If someone in the house had measles, whooping cough, mumps or small pox, the house was quarantined, with a coloured sign on the front door, meaning that no one could leave the grounds.

People with serious diseases would be quarantined at the Isolation Hospital on the east side of the Don, just north of the Don Jail, known to local children as the "pest house". Visitors to a loved one could come only so close to the grounds, from which point they would have to throw their gifts to those on the inside.

When someone died, the blinds were drawn, a black sash was hung on the door, and the corpse would "lie in state" in the parlour while neighbours came in to pay their last respects. Eva Broomhall remembers that when her family first moved to Cabbagetown, to a small house in Wilkins Avenue, her mother gave birth to a girl, who died a short time later. Following tradition, white crepe was hung on the front door. Soon after, well-meaning neighbours, most of them total strangers, began coming into the house to see the baby. Eva Broomhall states that her mother was horrified by this experience, and the crepe was quickly removed. While it is easy to understand her feeling in such a situation, nonetheless it is clear that what happened was yet another example of the spirit of Cabbagetown, that neighbours rush to support and comfort those among them who suffer misfortune. It is this type of attitude which gave Cabbagetown its strength in the face of overwhelming adversity.

THE GREAT WAR

On August 4, 1914, Bill Hambly's Scout camp at Lake Couchiching was interrupted by news that Canada was at war. He remembers coming back to Toronto to witness the sight of torches being carried through the streets of Cabbagetown in an atmosphere of near hysteria. That night a mob stormed the Liederkranz Club, a previously popular German restaurant and beer garden on Richmond Street.

Cabbagetown, having been settled by immigrants from the British Isles, particularly Northern Ireland, was a bastion of British patriotism. The people of Cabbagetown may not have been unified in all respects, but it is clear that prevailing sentiment included an intense love for and loyalty to the British Royal family, the Empire, and, above Queen Street, at least, the Protestant Church. The attitude of patriotism felt by many Cabbagetowners for all things British explains why, as Max Walker describes it, "Cabbagetown produced more volunteer soldiers in two world wars than did any area of equal size." The former Dufferin School cadets, who as boys had paraded with antique rifles down University Avenue, rushed to sign up, to end this "phoney war", which most people felt would be over within a few weeks.

Women left their homes to take up work in factories, while recruiters set up stands on street corners, to take advantage of the wave of patriotism that enveloped Cabbagetown. Some of those who, to their sorrow, were not yet old enough to fight, signed up to assist in some way to support the war effort or "keep the home fires burning." Some of these, such as young Gordon Sinclair, signed up with the "S.O.S.", short for "Soldiers of the Soil", in which boys were sent out to work on farms while their owners went off to war. In his autobiography, he comments that the participants quickly adopted a new meaning for "S.O.S." in line with the work which they were really performing, as "shovellers of shit."

The boys who went to war—The First Rifle Corps, Dufferin School

—Dufferin School Old Boys' Association Year Book, 1931

During the war an even greater feeling of togetherness developed in Cabbagetown. Petty differences and racial and ethnic distinctions seemed to disappear, as people decided they had to work together for the common good. An example of this new feeling of harmony was the greatly decreased use of racial and ethnic nicknames. This feeling of camaraderie which thus developed became even stronger when black crepe began to appear on doorfronts, and military funerals began to wind their way up Parliament Street to St. James Cemetery. Park School and the old Toronto General Hospital were taken over for military purposes, as the realization dawned that this was no "phoney war" and that a great number of sons and daughters of Cabbagetown had left their homes never to return.

It seems to be generally agreed among oldtimers that the War put an abrupt end to the "golden years of Cabbagetown", from which the area never fully recovered. As Llewellyn Lewis puts it, "Cabbagetown died after the War." Whether this may have been a premature obituary for a durable tradition, remains to be seen.

Orange Lodge, Branch No. 1, July 12th, c. 1910

—*City of Toronto Archives, Ref. No. James Collection 668*

WHAT THEY THOUGHT

As already stated, the enormous response and sacrifice by Cabbage-town to the War effort was the natural outcome of a shared patriotism that was part of its fundamental spirit. This basic feeling of unity of purpose among Cabbagetowners managed to surpass some of the underlying divisive influences of religion and ethnic origin. However, these differences were real, and were not without their effect on the kaleidoscope of Cabbagetown life.

Religion was very much a part of life in Cabbagetown. It has been said that "Cabbagetown developed as the main reception area for Toronto's Irish Protestant population."[17] Assuming the boundaries of Cabbagetown to have been north of Queen Street, this was no doubt the case, because that part of Cabbagetown up to Gerrard was almost solidly Protestant, and it was in that part of the area that there developed the Northern Irish way of life which was very much an integral part of the spirit of Cabbagetown. It is often said that the south of Queen was called Corktown, due to the concentration of Southern Irish Roman Catholics who came there to settle around St. Paul's Church. This would, of course, tie in with the view of many Cabbagetowners that Queen Street was the southern boundary of Cabbagetown. In time, however, some of these initial mental barriers broke down, as people learned to live with each other and to fight common problems of disease, poverty and unemployment. Also, there were never such clear geographical barriers in any event. Trinity Church was, after all, well south of Queen Street, and there was quite a large community of both English and Scottish immigrants south of there as well. Physical boundary lines were blurred, as were religious ones, as shown by the fact that it was some of the most prominent Anglicans in the city who contributed funds for the building of the first St. Paul's Church, and the Roman Catholic-sponsored House of Providence, which looked after the need of so many non-Catholics that it became known as the "House of Protestants".

Ecumenicalism could, however, go only so far in Cabbagetown. For one of the most powerful organizations there, as in the rest of the city, was the Orange Order, whose fife and drum bands, while practising on Trefann Street, would "stray" down Power Street into the Catholic part of town, expecting a donnybrook, and getting it. For whatever harmony might exist between Roman Catholics and Protestants on other days of the year, March 17 and July 12 were quite different. Dorine Harrison remembers her father saying that the gang fights in Toronto in the 1960s could not compare with the

battles in Cabbagetwon on those dates during the early part of this century. Although there clearly was a significant amount of tolerance between the two groups at other times of the year, consciousness of religious grouping created ongoing tensions between them.

Yet another sector is heard from in the recollection of William Bremner that "going down Sackville Street you had to fight both ways; you had to fight when you hit Queen and Sackville with the regular Roman Catholics, and further down with the French Catholics," (this referring to a French community that grew up around Queen and Sumach). The fact that children fought over such things indicates that the religious and other differences between the two groups, while it may have been forgotten from time to time during periods of common emergency, never disappeared altogether.

There were pervasive religious influences in Cabbagetown life other than those involving Protestant-Catholic dissension. In fact, Cabbagetown was full of churches and missions, most of them with roots going well back into Victorian times. Few of the original churches still survive, but some of the oldest, such as Trinity, St. Paul's, St. Peter's, and St. Batholomew's, do remain, and will be described in more detail later in the book. One well-known Cabbagetown church which no longer exists, was St. Giles Presbyterian, on Oak Street. Mary McKeown now possesses a newel post taken from the church after the final service held just before it was turned over to the wreckers. Maintaining that all of her years of touching that post on her way into Sunday School gave her as much right to the post as any wrecker, her mother instructed her now-grown daughter to conceal the post beneath her coat. On the way home she was offered a seat on the streetcar because of her "condition".

There was also one Jewish synogogue in Cabbagetown, on Berkeley Street, just north of Queen, known as the Bnai Israel Hamizrachim Congregation.

Cabbagetown also appears to have been a hotbed of evangelism, with preachers setting up tents at Riverdale Park, or holding prayer meetings at the fundamentalist Parliament Street Methodist Church. Connie Smith remembers that the representatives of the Yonge Street Mission used to come on Sunday afternoons in a large van, and carry on mission services on Carlton Street just south of the Riverdale Zoo. They gave out free Bibles, and the services were conducted by a saintly-looking old gentleman by the name of Mr. Davies.

For most people in Cabbagetown, life centred around the church, and most old timers seem to agree that, while there were differences among people of different faiths, there was generally a peaceful coexistence.

Notwithstanding the generally British White Anglo-Saxon Protestant nature of most of Cabbagetown, there was also a sprinkling of immigrants from other national or ethnic backgrounds. There were a number of Jewish people, some of whom operated the corner stores. There were also Macedonians, Bulgarians, and French. The somewhat ambivalent attitude to this situation, as expressed by old-time Cabbagetowners to-day, is expressed in the following statement of Max Walker:

> I am not a racist, but in those days a Jew was a yid, an Englishman a limey, a German a hieney, an Italian a wop, a Frenchman a frog, a Hungarian a hunkie, a Pole a polock, a Ukranian a uke. Sure there were plenty of fights at Jarvis based primarily on racial differences, but everyone emerged stronger for learning to respect the good qualifications in one another.

Most of the Cabbagetown old-timers, almost all of whom, it appears, are White Anglo-Saxon Protestants, seem convinced that although words such as the above and others like them were used frequently, and fights often developed over them among children, nevertheless all nationalities "got along well." In contrast to this is a Jewish old-timer, who says that there was anti-semitism, particularly against small businessmen, in the 1930s and 1940s. Children would go to bar mitzvah classes through back alleys to avoid the names, taunts and physical abuse hurled at them by members of non-Jewish national groups. It is clear that at least for some minority groups in Cabbagetown the environment was to some extent a hostile one.

The political lines in Cabbagetown seem also to be somewhat confused, but there is no doubt as to the political stripe of the great majority of Cabbagetowners. Charles Dickens, after visiting Toronto, wrote:

> The wild and rabid Toryism of Toronto is, I speak seriously, appalling."

This "appalling Toryism", traces of which may still be seen to-day, seems to have been part of the accepted Cabbagetown outlook on life, at least north of Queen Street. To Orange Cabbagetown, the devotion to one King and one Flag, one God and the British Empire was naturally and inextricably woven into the concept, "and one Party!"

In general, it is probably fair to say, as has been said, by Hugh Garner[18], that Cabbagetowners believed in God, the Royal family, the Conservative Party and private enterprise; and that they were "generally unskilled working people, . . . suspicious and condescending to all heathen religions, higher education, "foreigners" and social reformers."

HOW THEY ENTERTAINED THEMSELVES

Life in Cabbagetown was not always grim. In fact, the difficulties which Cabbagetowners encountered in many aspects of their life made it that much more necessary that they enjoy themselves when they got the chance. And they certainly seemed to know how to enjoy themselves, but, unlike today, more often as participants than spectators. Even during the Depression, when the feeling of the times was generally pessimistic, the residents of Cabbagetown got together to make their own fun and, at least temporarily, banish the blues.

From the earliest days of settlement in the Cabbagetown area there have been some activities generally common to all periods of history. During the days of the Town of York, people would wander over to the spacious grounds of Moss Park, near Sherbourne and Queen, for sports events, picnics, and other social gatherings.

During the same period, a Fair Green was laid out on the south side of Front just west of Berkeley, at which were held cattle shows, wild beast shows and circuses. In 1852, P.T. Barnum's Grand Colossal Museum and Menagerie came to the Fair Green, with elephants, lions, a "sacred Burmese bull", and the special attraction, "General" Tom Thumb, who, at age twenty is said to have been twenty-eight inches high and weighed fifteen pounds. The Fair Green was also a site where the militia drilled from time to time, and it was used as a mustering ground for large parades such as the Orangemen's Parade on July 12. From the Fair Green one could also, if one wanted, watch the public hangings of prisoners at the jail to the east.

Winter sports were popular in the Town of York. In the winter, less work could be done, so there was more time for leisure activities, which might include curling, skating, log-sawing, target-shooting, wrestling, snow-shoeing, tobogganing, ice-racing, ice-sailing, and hockey. Curling was played on the Don as early as 1829, and by 1837 the first curling club had been established. Somewhat later (1890), a curling rink was established at the south east corner of Prospect and Ontario, with a skating rink beside it. Another skating rink was the Victoria Rink at the south west corner of Gerrard and Sherbourne, where, in 1862, the first "grand prize skating matches" were held. In 1881-84 there was a skating rink on Parliament Street south of Oak. In 1890 there was one at the south east corner of Ontario and Wellesley, near the site of an organ factory which had been established there six years before.

From Mrs. Simcoe's time onward, people skated on the Don.

Skating at Moss Park, Shuter Street, c. 1905

—*A Post Card*

Another event there, recorded during the 1870s, was the turkey shoot, where for twenty-five cents participants were given a chance of procuring their Christmas dinner, meaning whatever was left of the turkey after it was shot.

Other popular pastimes, still common during the later years of Cabbagetown, were going for sleigh rides in the winter, or ice-boating on a frozen Toronto bay. In the 1930s, an iceboat ride would cost twenty-five cents for adults, fifteen cents for children. There was also a peculiar contraption, called a "cigar-boat" that plied the waters of the bay.

There were lots of other forms of entertainment available to Cabbagetowners in the 1920s and 1930s. One of the most popular was going to movies. Some of the popular theatres in the area were the Bluebell (south east Parliament and Dundas, now called the Break

dance), the Eclipse (Parliament, south of Gerrard), the Parliament (Parliament north of Spruce), the Carlton (Parliament, north of Carlton, now the C.B.C. Studio), the Imperial, later known as the Rialto (Queen Street just west of Tracy now the Good Shepherd Refuge), the Teck, (a few doors west of Broadview on Queen), and the Idle Hour (Queen Street, west of Trefann). Among these, only the Bluebell is still a movie theatre.

The Imperial was owned by St. Paul's Church, and on Fridays Dean Hand, of the Church, let the Roman Catholic children in free. The Parliament was also known as the B and F Parliament, standing for Bloom and Fine. Admission to all theatres was five cents, or a few cents more on nights when they gave away dishes. The children, particularly, liked the Saturday matinees, when a musician with a piano and other sound effects would add an extra thrill to

The Teck Theatre, north side of Queen Street East, just west of Broadview Avenue, 1932. At the time the Broadview House was known as the Lincoln Hotel.

—City of Toronto Archives Ref: Salmon Collection 641

The Eclipse Theatre, 387-93 Parliament Street, at 10:10 a.m. on July 27th, 1949. — *City of Toronto 9.2.36 795 Parliament St. Print 38*

The Imperial Movie Theatre and Vaudeville House, north-west corner of Queen Street East and Tracy Streets, 1919. The building, owned by the Roman Catholic Church, later became the Good Shepherd Refuge. — *City of Toronto Archives, Ref: Salmon Collection 825*

the *Perils of Pauline*, or a Tom Mix movie. Other popular movies starred Lassie, the current Tarzan, Tom Mix, Art Accord, Harry Carey, William S. Hart, Hoot Gibson, John Bunny, Marie Dressler, Mack Sennett, Harold Lloyd, Harry Langdon, Charlie Chaplin or Mary Pickford. Some of the best-known movies of the period were *The Poor Little Rich Girl, The Birth of a Nation, Pearl White,* and an early two-reel version of *Dr. Jekyll and Mr. Hyde.* If a child was lucky, he or she might be taken downtown to see a movie at Shea's in the Strand. For adults, there were also burlesque houses, such as the Star, on Temperance Street, or the Gaiety, on Richmond.

For outdoor entertainment, families might attend band concerts in City parks, which were free in the summer, or perhaps five cents when they were held indoors at the Moss Park or Broadview rinks. Or they could go to Scarborough Beach Park, Sunnyside or Hanlan's Point, all of which had large amusement parks. For a quieter time, they could look at the flowers at Allan Gardens or stroll through Riverdale Park.

There were many sporting events available both for spectators and participants. Many of these have already been described in a previous section. Professional lacrosse was played at Hanlan's Point and Scarborough Beach Park. A keen rivalry developed between the Torontos, owned by R.J. Fleming, and the Tecumsehs. It was at that time that R.J. Fleming, who also operated the Toronto Street Railway,

decided to allow to ride free anyone carrying a lacrosse stick. Bill Hambly recalls that his father kept the family well supplied with lacrosse sticks by bringing home the broken ones from his team, the Tecumsehs.

Although the professional Toronto baseball team no longer played there, the field north of the Sunlight Soap plant, south of Queen on the other side of the Don, was the site for amateur and semi-professional ball. The small street, Baseball Place, is the only memento of the baseball stadium which once stood there.

Boxing was a popular sport with Cabbagetowners. Local boxers worked out of the Classic or Union Jack Athletic Clubs, or St. Paul's Boxing Club. Charles Murphy remembers running boxing matches in the 1930s. He was the 1931 fly-weight champion of Ontario and the 1935 Canadian Champion. He retired as an amateur after thirty-four matches, turned professional in 1935, and went to England to fight. He was listed in Ripley's *Believe it or Not* as the tallest fly-weight ever.

His partner, John Palmer, was the 1930 bantam weight champion of Ontario. Other successful Cabbagetown boxers were Jack

Johnson, who fought "Kid" Chocolate from Cuba for the World Champion feather-weight crown, (he lost); and Albert "Frenchie" Belanger, who was the world champion fly-weight boxer in 1927, and was inducted into the Canadian Sports Hall of Fame in 1963. Charles Murphy says that Belanger was probably the only Cabbage-towner to make real money from boxing in those days—some ninety thousand dollars during his career. Another Cabbagetowner, Larry Gains, a black man, was the British Empire heavy-weight champion.

From time to time the circus came to town, setting up on the Don flats. Gordon Sinclair remembers when the Buffalo Bill show came to Toronto, and he was hired to carry water to the horses, which were stabled behind the gum factory on Logan. There, he says, he met Buffalo Bill, whom he found to be enormously fat and apparently drunk most of the time.

In those days, before many people had radios, one often made one's own entertainment, and simple get-togethers with friends were often the most enjoyed of all forms of leisure time activity. On Saturday night people often had parties to which everyone brought food, and there would be singing and dancing, (but no liquor), throughout the evening. Some people had garden parties, (also called "house parties" or "block parties") where everyone was charged a small sum to help pay the rent. Such parties were held at Tree's estate, on Sherbourne Street in Moss Park. The charge was five cents to get in and five cents for ice cream.

The men liked to gather to "chew the fat" at the firehall on Dundas Street at Parliament, or at Harry's barber shop at Gerrard and Ontario, where each would have his own shaving mug.

Each year people would flock to see the Orangemen's parade. Also, before the First World War, a German brass band used to come to street corners in Cabbagetown where they would play in return for change. From time to time evangelists would bring various entertainers with them to add "colour" to their preaching.

People enjoyed going to amateur hours at local schools, Wilfred Parkin remembers that the audience would throw tomatoes at performers trying to sing, make birdcall imitations or dance the Charleston. The prize for the winner was five dollars, but in many cases the crowd would call "Get the hook", and a long hook would come out from the wings and drag the unfortunate competitor off the stage.

The Hotel Gerrard, at the south-east corner of Parliament and Gerrard, in 1919. Certainly the largest and most modern hotel built in Cabbagetown in this century, it rivalled the Winchester in the level of excellence with which it treated its guests.
—City of Toronto Archives Salmon 1134

DRINKING IN OLD CABBAGETOWN

From the earliest days, liquor was readily obtainable. In 1856 it was reported that there were over five hundred licensed and unlicensed houses selling intoxicating drinks—and this in a city with a population of only forty thousand souls! In that year it was record-ed that one out of every nine citizens had been brought before a police magistrate for drunkenness. Statistics were also gathered showing that 1085 men, 526 women and 175 persons under twenty had been declared drunkards by habit and repute. In those days a drunk would be committed to gaol for one month.

With the English and Irish backgrounds of so many of her citizens, Cabbagetown had its fair share of drinking places. Those street corners that didn't have grocery stores housed establishments to serve the drinking needs of the thirsty populace. Many of these commenced operation in Cabbagetown's early period, and one, the Derby Tavern, at King and Parliament, built and in operation in 1846, can lay claim to being the oldest tavern in the city, (with apologies to the Wheat Sheaf, (1849)).

Don Vale House, Winchester Street, East of the Necropolis, 1848-1876.   —*Robertson's Landmarks of Toronto, Volume III opp. p. 302, 1898*

Supplies for the pubs were, of course, readily available, with the largest brewery and distillery in British North America (Gooderham & Worts) just at the bottom of Mill Street (now Trinity), and most of the large Toronto breweries either within the boundaries of Cabbagetown or not far from them.

The pubs were certainly popular, and many a wife had to meet her husband at the factory gate to make sure that the proceeds from his meagre pay cheque were not distributed to the proprietors of the several corner drinking establishments that he would pass on his way home. Some of these proprietors, particularly during the Depression, when they were as desperate as everyone else, would stand on the sidewalk in front of their pubs and try to steer customers in through the doors. In some cases, the menacing appearance of some of these barkeepers, and the forcefulness with which they tried to persuade the passing workers, amounted to downright intimidation.

Members of the "temperance" movement, who succeeded in bringing about Prohibition in 1916, were constantly involved in pressuring authorities to make the hotels licensed for the sale of alcoholic beverages actually "keep hotel".

This was, of course, in variance with the true operation of many establishments, whose only goal in life was to "keep bar", although there were a few quite nice and respectable hotels, such as the Gerrard and the Winchester.

The following list, for the year, 1912, shows the hotels existing in that time in the Cabbagetown area;

Broadview House	N.W. Queen and Broadview
Dominion House	N.W. Queen and Sumach
Hotel Beresford	Queen near Seaton
Hotel Gerrard	S.E. Gerrard and Parliament
Hotel Rupert	N.W. Queen and Parliament
Hotel Winchester	S.E. Parliament and Winchester
King Edward Hotel Annex	157 Sherbourne Street
Kormann House	S.E. Queen and Sherbourne
National Hotel	S.E. King and Sherbourne
Princess Hotel	N.E. Queen and Princess
Shamrock Hotel	S.E. Gerrard and River
Sherbourne House	S.W. Sherbourne and Richmond
Victor Inn	284 King Street East
Wilton House	N.E. Dundas and Ontario
Wrights	S.E. King and Parliament

The following are brief sketches of a few of the better known taverns in Cabbagetown:

Derby Tavern
A long frontage on King Street where it slants to the north-east from Parliament to meet Queen at the Don, and a peculiar roofline, are about the only outward distinguishing characteristics of what is probably the oldest tavern in Toronto still operating in its original building. The place exudes mustiness and old age. It would appear that this building was erected in the period 1846-47. There was certainly a pub in operation there in those years, and since. The first innkeeper was William Wright. Subsequently it has been known by various names, including the Welcome Home, Oriental, and, finally, since 1941, the Derby.

Rupert Hotel
Built in the late 1870s, the Rupert Hotel, at the north west corner of Queen and Parliament, the main intersection of Cabbagetown, had a livery stable beside it and was considered one of the better establishments. It was known by Wilfred Parkin for its "stand-up bar, no women; with a short bald bartender and brass-handled pull taps." He says it was a source of entertainment for local chidren to go to the Rupert to watch the fights outside on the sidewalk. A local rowdy named Tom Downs once handcuffed a policeman to a lamp-post when the officer tried to arrest him. Originally the Elephant and Castle, then the John O'Neil Hotel, the Rupert was so named in about 1912. The building is no longer a hotel, but the original sign, "Rupert Hotel", painted over but easily readable, still hangs on the second floor wall on the Parliament Street side.

Don Vale House
Known as a "frequent resort of the sporting fraternity" the Don Vale House stood down in the Don Valley on the north side of Winchester Street, (then known as the plank road), at the foot of the hill of the Necropolis, from the late 1840s to about 1875-76, when it was pulled down. Cock fights and boxing matches were staged at its various out-buildings by the "sporting men" of the day. Its only claim to the historical significance is that it provides some justification for the decision by City planners, reporting on the Don Planning District in 1965-66, to apply the name Don Vale to the area bounded by the St. James Cemetery, Parliament, Gerrard, Riverdale Park and the Necropolis Cemetery. In fact, Don Vale is probably, for this reason, a historically more appropriate name for this area than is the now-accepted Cabbagetown.

The Winchester
Occupying a commanding position at south east Parliament and Winchester Streets, the Winchester, formerly the Lake View, was in 1885 termed "one of the pleasantest public resorts in the east end of the City". Although a predecessor, first known as the Santa Claus, occupied this site in the 1860s, the present buildings date from 1881, in the case of Winchester Hall on the Winchester side, and 1888, in the case of the large central building on Parliament Street. A plaque on the wall to the north side still bears the name "Winchester Hall". With a high lantern, or monitor, at the top of its tower, which once bore a high flagpole, the Winchester could be seen from many parts of the City.

It had all the most modern conveniences. In 1891, it had electric bells, bathrooms on every flat, telephones, and iron and patent rope fire escapes. It featured good access to streetcars (a line ran up Parliament and along Winchester to the Riverdale Zoo); a large commodious lodgeroom and public hall, where several friendly societies held meetings; a pleasant summer garden, a billiard room; and bowling alleys. In those days, the red brick was allowed to show on the handsome walls of the old hotel, Winchester and Parliament were paved with cedar block, and a horse trough stood on Winchester. Later, a portico was built out over the sidewalk from the Winchester entrance. The biggest crowd in its history jammed the drinking rooms on the last day before Prohibition came into effect, in 1916. In the eleven dry years that followed, the Winchester

The Winchester Hotel, (then known as the 'Lake View'), South-East corner, Parliament and Winchester Streets, 1891.
Toronto—Old and New, by G. Mercer Adam, 1891 The Mail Publishing Co.

managed to survive under the management of Mickey Wilson, through the rental of rooms and the operation of a dining room and an old-fashioned ice-cream parlour.

To-day the faded Winchester has lost most of its glory, but the high ornamental tin ceilings in its kitchen, and most of the original appearance of its upper floors, including gas light fixtures, have managed to survive. Potentially the most prominent and handsome building on Parliament and a prime candidate for the focal point of a rejuvenated commercial area there, the Winchester seems to be crying out desperately for help.

Dominion House

A handsome Romanesque building erected in 1891, a date which shows in a monogram on one side of the door, the Dominion House

"Hotel Rupert" sign at the N.W. corner of Parliament and Queen streets.
—George H. Rust-D'Eye

anchored the west end of the block on Queen at Sumach, the rest of which was covered by the substantial red-brick bulk of its sister the Dominion Brewery, erected in 1879-80. The Dominion had a long stand-up bar, and featured barrels covered with leather tops, as tables. Under the direction of its owner Alberta Crittall Shore, the Dominion was one of the first to go back into business when Premier Mitchell Hepburn decided to issue licences to hotels after the end of Prohibition.

Alberta Shore was a hard-headed business person and a flamboyant character on the Toronto scene. She kept the hotel rooms decorated in the Victorian style, with hundreds of bits of ornamental bric-a-brac. She made good investments and commanded the respect of her staff and of the men with whom she did business. She managed through these means to amass an estate worth one million dollars by the time she died, in 1955. She was also a famous figure for fashions, often appearing at social occasions wearing fabulously expensive jewels, hats and furs. Once she made a public appearance wearing rings worth more than fifty thousand dollars. Known as the "Grand Old Lady" she was an organizer and founder of the Ontario Hotel Association and gave generously to the needy in the Sackville Street area.

59

Avion Hotel

Located in a building erected in about 1890 at the north east corner of Gerrard and Sumach, the Avion was one of the hotels which opened after Prohibition had ended, when beer was selling for ten cents for a ten ounce draught, and a full bottle cost twenty cents. During the 1930's, waiters made about fifteen dollars a week, and most of the houses in the area, worth then about three thousand dollars to four thousand dollars, were owner-occupied. The Avion was built as a grocery store and for many years was the well-known Cruttenden's Pharmacy. Lately it has been re-named the Cabbagetown.

Shamrock Hotel

Known originally as the Farmers House, the Shamrock was situated at the south east corner of River and Gerrard streets. Known as a "working man's pub", it is remembered for other reasons by Mary MacKeown, whose grandfather used to go there to get a bucket of oysters for Saturday dinner, while her mother found it a good source of supply for empty cigar boxes. When the Regent Park housing development went up in the early 1950s, the Shamrock moved its name to Coxwell and Gerrard Streets.

WHERE BEER WAS MADE

As mentioned above, many of the large brewery buildings established in Toronto in the last century were built in Cabbagetown. This seems appropriate, since beer or malt liquor, was originally considered the drink of lower income groups, and soldiers. Of course, the primary importance of the breweries in this area was that they provided a source of income for the inhabitants of Cabbagetown throughout its history, except during Prohibition. Here is a brief description of a few of them:

1. Kormann Brewery (1864)

Situated at south west Richmond and Sherbourne, its predecessor, Hendersons, was Toronto's first brewery, established in 1815. By 1894, it was producing twenty-five thousand barrels of beer per year.

2. Bloor Brewery (1833)

It was built in the ravine between Sherbourne and Huntley Streets to tap the water of Severn Creek, the name, at that time, of the creek which ran down the Rosedale Valley, formerly Castle Frank Creek. Its founder was Joseph Bloor, one of the founders of Yorkville. In 1837 a blockhouse was built nearby, at the corner of Bloor and Sherbourne, which overlooked the brewery buildings.

3. Copland's Brewery

Also known as East Toronto Brewing, it was established in the 1840s on Parliament, south of Derby, by William Copland. By 1891, it occupied over five acres, and had probably the most extensive vaults and cellar in the city. In 1946 it was taken over by Labatt's and closed down.

4. Wood and Anderson

A small brewery which operated near the Necropolis Cemetery in the 1840s, it was owned by John Ward, who later took over the Don Vale House. It was torn down in 1860.

5. Don Brewery

Founded in the 1850s by Thomas Davies, the Don Brewery stood on the Don, east of River Street north of Queen. It was considered modern and efficient because it used water from the City waterworks, so it didn't need its own pump. Several of its large brick buildings still exist behind the newer Queen City Vinegar Company Building at 19 River Street.

6. Reinhardt's East End Brewery

Founded in 1862 by a Mr. Defries, it stood at the end of Mark Street, then Blevins Avenue, at the Don, until the building, no longer used for a brewery, burned down in the 1950s. It also used city watermains for water to brew its "XXX" ales and porters. Its' owner, H. Reinhardt, first introduced the manufacture of lager beer to Toronto.

7. Ontario Brewing and Malting Co.

Established in 1882 at 281-89 King Street East, it was originally known as the Queen City Malting Company, (The name Queen City seems to have been applied to Toronto since at least as early as 1860, possibly because of the celebrated visit to Toronto of the Prince of Wales in that year). In 1883 the Company exported 216,000 bushels of malt to the United States.

8. Dominion Brewery

A magnificent red and white brick block on the north side of Queen near Sumach, the Dominion was built in 1879-80, by Robert Davies, known as the most extensive exhibitor of Canadian ales and porters in foreign countries. Bill Hambly remembers that the Dominion had a brewmaster who weighed 350 pounds, and who when he died, needed a specially built casket in which to bury him. He also remembers one of the great sights of Cabbagetown, seeing the brewery carts, bearing kegs of beer on the sides, rumbling out of the gangway drawn by the Dominion's beautiful horses.

The building is a large and striking example of High Victorian architecture, with high mansarded towers, dormers and high quality

The Dominion Brewery, and Dominion House Tavern, Queen Street East, near Sumach, c. 1931. The buildings still exist, and have just been cleaned

—Toronto—An Illustrated Tour through its Highways and Byways c.1931

decorative brick work. Listed by the Toronto Historical Board for its architectural and contextual significance, it has just undergone a stunning transformation during its current renovation by Revenue Properties Co. Ltd., involving the cleaning of the brickwork on its whole southern front. This facade, and the great towers of the building, are to be preserved in this ambitious project, which is intended to produce 186,000 square feet of commercial space.

It is interesting to note the apparent impact of the building on the neighbourhood around it. A large number of labourers' houses, (including "Davies Terrace, 1877" at 467-77 Queen Street), were built in the immediate area during the later 1870s and early 1880s, many of them having similar architecture and brickwork to the Dominion Brewery Building.

Gooderham & Worts Distillery, c. 1890,
by A.H. Hider, Toronto Litho. Co.

—*Advertising Poster*

63

GOODERHAM AND WORTS

An important early business in operation at the south end of the Park, was the windmill of James Worts and William Gooderham, established in 1832. Today, the company is among the oldest continuously-operating business concerns in the city, and the Gooderham and Worts distillery complex is probably Canada's best-preserved group of Victorian industrial buildings.

The founders of the firm had a family, as well as business, relationship, since James Worts was married to Elizabeth Gooderham, sister to William. In 1831, James Worts arrived in Canada and came to the Town of York to find a place to erect a flour or grist mill. The mill was to be powered by wind, the main source in that part of England from which he had come. He chose a site in the bush, toward the south east corner of the present site in an area known at the time as Vale Pleasant.

The foundation was laid for the windmill in 1831. On July 25, 1832, William Gooderham, who had been a financing partner with his brother-in-law from the start, arrived in York, bringing with him fifty-three relatives and more money than the Bank of Upper Canada had ever before seen a customer deposit. It is likely that some of the relatives were skilled in building and operating mills. The area around the mill soon became a flourishing suburb. In 1832, the 71-foot-high windmill was completed by the partnership, known originally as "Worts and Gooderham, Millers", with an address of Wind Mills, Upper Canada. The mill commenced production on July 27, 1832, as a grist mill, and various grains were ground. Flour production commenced on October 5, 1832. Although the mill produced 293 barrels of flour in its first two months, it was soon realized that wind was not the best source of power. It was was so strong that it almost demolished the vanes, and within a year it was decided that an engine would be installed. It was also decided to erect a distillery, a common addition to a mill, since the mush and middlings which were by-products to the milling of grain, could be converted to whisky (with the residue to be sold as swine and cattle feed). The distillery was thus originally considered incidental to the mill.

By 1834, the windmill had become a landmark, which, with its nearby blockhouse erected a few years before, was featured prominently in many of the early pictures of the Town of York. The area became known as Windmill Point. In that year James Worts died, apparently by drowning himself, two weeks after his wife's death in childbirth, and the company's name was changed to simply William Gooderham.

By 1835, the sails had been removed or blown away, and a steam engine was in full operation. In 1837, a distillery went into operation, which would, by 1860, become the largest distillery in Canada, and one of the largest in the world, consuming annually 500,000 bushels of corn, 100,000 bushels of rye, 51,000 bushels of barley and 25,000 bushels of oats. It imported 8,000 tons of coal annually. It produced over 2 million gallons of spirits a year, which sold initially for the royal sum of fifty cents per gallon. In 1838, the company also became capable of producing malt.

By 1845, the top had blown off the old windmill. In that year, William Gooderham took in a new partner, James Gooderham Worts, his nephew and the son of his former partner, and the company name was changed to City of Toronto Steam Mills and Distillery, but the name Gooderham and Worts was also reinstituted and used by the company as its brand name. The partners were to continue in operation together for another thirty-five years.

By 1861, the distillery was completed, and another sideline had been developed. Although a short-lived small dairy had been set up in 1843, most of the slop from the distillery was sold as cattle feed to others. In 1861, stables were erected where one thousand cattle were fattened on slop piped under Trinity Street.

In 1859, Gooderham and Worts built a large gray distillery building. Its walls were of Kingston limestone, and it incorporated a grist mill and grain elevator at its east end and a distillery apparatus at the west end, in a manner similar to that followed in eighteenth and early nineteenth century English river mill buildings. It was designed by architect David Roberts, Sr.

The windmill was finally demolished in 1856. By then the original buildings had been joined by a number of others; and the entire complex, including William Gooderham's large house just south of Mill Street west of Trinity, occupied nine acres of land. Other buildings included a cooperage, malt houses, bottling rooms and cattle barns. On October 26, 1869 a disastrous fire, probably started by the sparks from a passing train, consumed most of the Gooderham and Worts buildings. The internal structure of the distillery building was destroyed, but was rebuilt, probably under the direction of architect David Roberts, Jr. who, with his father, did most of the architectural work for the Gooderham family. Most of the other buildings in the present complex date from the period immediately after the fire. The entire complex is listed by the Toronto Historical Board as an historic site.

William Gooderham and James Gooderham Worts were among the most prominent men in Toronto during the period 1845 to 1880. William Gooderham was the President of the Bank of Toronto. Both he and J.G. Worts were involved in many financial, industrial and religious organizations, and were major contributors to and wardens of Trinity Church for almost forty years. Both lived in large estates of land just north of the distillery. Their head office building, known to most Torontonians as the "flatiron building", stands at the corner of Front, Wellington and Church. They were buried, side by side, in St. James Cemetery.

As a postscript, the windmill that they built became a marker for surveys of Toronto, a reference point that remained long after the windmill itself had gone.

THE INSTITUTIONS OF CABBAGETOWN

THE CHURCHES

Trinity Church

Trinity Church, also known as "Little Trinity" the "Church in the Park", and the "Poor Man's Church", is the oldest church building in Toronto. It was built in 1843, at the south west corner of King and Trinity Streets, to the design of architect Henry Bower Lane.

After St. James Cathedral had burned down in 1839, it was realized that there was a very great need for a second Anglican Church, particularly one which would serve the poor members of the Protestant Irish settlement east of Parliament, who couldn't afford the pew rents at St. James'. A protest parade and demonstration, on July 12, 1842, brought forth assistance from Bishop Strachan, who arranged to acquire land for the church, and from some affluent and prominent men, such as Enoch Turner, William Gooderham, James Gooderham Worts, chief Justice John Beverley Robinson and Joseph Shuter, who raised funds to build the church.

The funds were raised, the church was built, and on February 18, 1844 Bishop Strachan dedicated the church and preached the first sermon. Trinity was to serve a parish bounded by Queen, Sherbourne, the Don River and the bay, an area which traditionally had housed the poor.

The building is of red brick, with white brick buttresses. Its eighty foot-high tower was originally intended to bear a thirty foot spire, but the parish never raised enough money to build one. The church was built to seat 400 people, with free seating accommodation for strangers. It originally had a gallery. The interior and furnishings were severe and simple. Its architectural style has been described as "undecorated perpendicular 13th century Gothic", also as "Tudor Gothic", "late Regency", and "early Victorian". It was built at the height of the Gothic revival, when churches and other buildings were being patterned after medieval English churches.

Trinity Church came to be known as "Little Trinity", to distinguish it from Holy Trinity, which was built four years later. The widow of Rev. Ripley, who died in 1849 during the epidemic of cholera and typhus which swept the area, donated a silver communion service to the church in his memory. Shortly after, it disappeared, only to be found in 1933 by a cleaner at Holy Trinity. Although badly tarnished, it was cleaned and returned, with great ceremony, to Trinity Church.

Trinity also became known as the "Poor People's Church", for obvious reasons. In 1923, it was written: "To-day "Little Trinity" is in an unsavoury neighborhood and the rector has an infinite opportunity of being Elder Brother of the Poor; ..."[19]

In 1961, Trinity Church was badly damaged by a fire, but the citizens of Toronto raised funds in the amount of $230,000 for its restoration.

Both Trinity Church and its handsome late Georgian rectory, built in 1853, are listed by the Toronto Historical Board.

The oldest parishioner of Trinity Church is Mrs. Jane Richmond Chambers, who was baptized in the church in 1885. Her family has been associated with Little Trinity since the 1870s. At the present time, five generations of the Chambers family, including former Fire Chief Charles Chambers, worship at Trinity Church.

St. Paul's Roman Catholic Church

This magnificent Italian Renaissance-style church was erected in 1887 just south of Queen on Power Street, which was named for the first bishop of western Ontario. The parish dates back to 1822, when the land was purchased for the church. Recently, in June 1982, the congregation held a birthday celebration to mark the 160 years of St. Paul's.

In 1821, the Roman Catholic congregation of Toronto was authorized to sell their lot at George and Adelaide Streets, (later the site of the Bank of Upper Canada), and purchase land "in a more eligible situation" in or near the centre of the Town of York. Consequently, the site of St. Paul's was purchased in 1822. The population of the Town of York in that year was 1,336.

In 1826, Upper Canada became a diocese, the first diocese to be established in a British Dominion since the Reformation. It was called the Diocese of Kingston, and Father Macdonell a former Scottish highland priest, became its first bishop. In that year the first Roman Catholic church erected in this city, and the only church of any description east of Jarvis Street, was built on this site. The Church at that time had a heavy debt, but it managed to pull through with the help of contributions from some of the leading Protestants of the community such as Attorney-General Clark, Dr.

Pieta at St. Paul's Church, Power Street, dedicated to the memory of Bishop Power and the immigrants who died in 1847 and were buried in the adjacent churchyard.

—George H. Rust-D'Eye

Interior of St. Paul's Roman Catholic Church, Power Street

—Panda Associates

Widmer, Robert Baldwin and Samuel P. Jarvis.

The 1826 church was a substantial brick building with a tessellated ("having a finely chequered surface") pattern of bricks. It was regarded as the most handsome church in the Town of York.

In 1841, a new diocese was created, including all of Upper Canada west of Newcastle. Father Michael Power was appointed its first bishop, and he chose Toronto as his espicopal seat. Thus St. Paul's became the cathedral church of the diocese of Toronto, a position it would hold until 1848, when St. Michael's Cathedral opened.

The purchase of land for St. Michael's was arranged by Bishop Power, who realized that the one priest at St. Paul's was hardly enough for the rapidly expanding parish of three thousand (out of thirteen thousand in Toronto). He ran into some difficulty in choosing the site, because many people felt that the corner of what is now Shuter and Bond Streets was too far out in the suburbs. He did manage to choose the name for the new cathedral, which he called after his own name-saint. However, he did not live to see it dedicated, for he died while ministering to one of his parishioners, struck down by fever brought by the many Irish immigrants who were flooding into the area around St. Paul's. His funeral was held at St. Paul's, and his body lies under a vault beneath the high altar at St. Michael's.

In 1879, Rt. Rev. Timothy O'Mahoney arrived from Australia, by way of Rome, to take over as bishop of St. Paul's. Under his direction, plans for a new church were formed, and in 1887 the ground-breaking ceremony was held. Bishop O'Mahoney worked hard to raise $100,000 for his great dream, and on December 22, 1889, it was dedicated to God by the Bishop of Kingston. The strain was too hard on Bishop O'Mahoney however, and within three years he was dead.

The first Roman Catholic cemetery in Toronto was established in the 1850s in the church yard around St. Paul's. All but one of the graves which were placed there have since been removed. However, just to the right of the stairs before you enter St. Paul's, lies the body of Bishop O'Mahoney, watching over the church which was his dream.

The building was designed by architect Joseph Connelly. It is in the symbolic cruciform shape typical of many churches, and seats 1,250 plus another 100 in the basement. Its campanile, or Italianate tower, is 129 feet high. At the top of it hangs the original bell from the 1826 cathedral.

Eric Arthur has described St. Paul's in the following words:

> This church was a rather courageous attempt at a design in the Italian Renaissance manner in a city where nearly all churches were Gothic...The interior is quite the most beautiful church interior in Toronto...[20]

Donald Jones, in several of his columns written for the Toronto Daily Star, has called it "one of the lost wonders" of this City.

Outside, the attractive Renaissance Romanesque walls are of Credit Valley sandstone and Cleveland limestone. The front facade especially, is a striking and unusual joy to behold. But it is when one enters St. Paul's that the awesome splendour of this building is suddenly realized. For inside it is like a European church, with a rich and sunny atmosphere. The high vaulted ceiling and rows of graceful white columns with intricately carved Ionic capitals, and the large light-filled windows under richly decorated concave recesses, all contribute to a feeling of amazement and awe, in a way which few other buildings in Toronto can even approach.

Aside from the sculpture which is the building itself, St. Paul's Church interior is lavishly decorated, as well befits a Renaissance church. Above each column is a well crafted circular mosaic depiction of the head of one of the Apostles. The grand ceiling, in the style of the Sistine Chapel, is filled with gigantic paintings in the style of Michelangelo and Raphael depicting the life and death of St. Paul. They were painted during the 1911 improvements, by Signor Caroselli. Above the altar are striking paintings of the conversion of St. Paul and the Last Supper, executed in 1893. Along the sides of the aisles are exquisitely-carved stations of the cross. All of these features contribute to making St. Paul's the most outstanding Renaissance building in the City, and the most important architectural gem of Cabbagetown.

The House Of Providence

Associated with and supported by St. Paul's, and situated just to the south of it on Power Street, was the House of Providence, a building devoted to providing relief for the aged, orphans and the sick and destitute, without distinction as to creed. This was one of the most important agencies for social welfare in Cabbagetown and one of the earliest and largest charitable institutions in Ontario, opening in 1857. As already mentioned, the House of Providence, like the soup kitchens of St. Paul's, was totally non-denominational. Whoever came for help got served, as long as the food held out, a philosophy of caring totally typical of the Cabbagetown approach to life.

The House of Providence was also an architectural gem. Designed by architect William Hay, in the French Renaissance

St. Peter's Church, N.E. corner of Carlton and Bleecker

—Toronto in the Camera 1867

The House of Providence, Power Street, South of Queen Street East, shown in 1875.
— *Public Archives of Canada*

style, it looked like a fairy-tale castle whose proper setting would be in the French countryside. Exhibiting some of the characteristics of the High Victorian Second Empire school, its steep mansarded towers added a fanciful air, intended to uplift the spirits of the needy souls who came to its doors. The House of Providence was torn down rather recently to make way for the Richmond Street approach to the Don Valley Parkway.

St. Peter's Church

In 1864, the congregation which then held its services in the cemetery chapel of St. James-the-Less on Parliament, purchased land at the corner of Bleeker and Carlton Streets. In 1865, the corner stone was laid, and on June 10, 1966, the beautiful church of St. Peter was opened for service by Bishop John Strachan. The first minister of St. Peter's, and the incumbent for its first forty-two years, was Rev. Samuel Boddy, whose house, at 21 Winchester Street, still stands. The church experienced rapid growth. Its policy of offering free pews for evening services made it more accessible to less well-off members of the community. In 1872, transepts were added. In 1880 it underwent alterations to increase its seating capacity from four to six hundred. In 1880 the Sunday school building to the north was erected. The church quickly developed a good reputation and was associated with many charitable organizations. It had a thriving Sunday School. Max Walker remembers that "the church in the early twentieth century, was an integral part of society. St. Peter's was the focus for the social as well as the spiritual life of its parishioners".

The building, designed by Gundry and Langley, architects, was described as "modern English Gothic." The walls, both inside and out, rely for their effect on the contrasts created by red and white brick. At the west end, the bell turret springs from massive buttresses arched over the rose window. The roof is pierced by "dormerlets". They and the belfry were once surmounted by large ornamental vanes, or cresting, which were removed at one time because they were thought dangerous. Parts of the small ornate late Victorian iron fence, which once surrounded the church, still remain but are badly in need of repair.

A bizarre coincidence occurred early in the 1950s. On the day that Sacred Heart Roman Catholic Church half a block to the west re-opened its doors after renovation and repair work, the bell of St. Peter's fell from the tower, bounced down the roof and landed in the mud beside the church. It remains there to this day, and when last seen had flowers growing in it. Years later, when St. Enoch's Church was sold, St. Peter's purchased its bell, which can now be heard on Sunday mornings summoning people to its service.

The worst of a series of set fires, on May 3, 1973, caused great damage to St. Peter's, destroying the chancel, organ, and the windows over the Communion table and causing smoke damage to the rest of the church. A restoration appeal, led by Rev. George Harvie, managed to raise $43,000, and the building was cleaned and restored. On December 16, 1979, Lt.-Gov. Pauline McGibbon and a large congregation attended a service at St. Peter's to witness the unveiling of a Toronto Historical Board plaque.

St. Enoch's Presbyterian Church

A very handsome red brick Romanesque church stands at the north east corner of Winchester and Metcalfe Streets. It was built in 1891 by a congregation which had started out as a mission from St. Andrews Church and whose previous place of worship was a house at the south west corner of Sackville and Winchester. The church quickly built up a large Sunday School and became popular in the community. Max Walker recalls "Beautiful hymns were always heard. It became a neighbourhood playhouse for the community."

In 1895, Rev. Alexander MacMillan, who lived at 152 Winchester Street, became the pastor of St. Enoch's. His son, Ernest, who played the organ at St. Enoch's, went on to become conductor of the Toronto Symphony Orchestra, and one of the greatest musicians Canada has ever produced.

St. Enoch's has seen a number of drastic changes in its use during this century. In 1939 it became a house of worship of the United Church, when its congregation merged with that of Gerrard Street United Church, a former Methodist congregation which began in 1878 as a mission church. Its last building, at the south west corner of Sumach and Spruce, built in 1923, was taken over in 1939 by the Gerrard Kiwanis Boys' Club. The fact of this merger explains the otherwise difficult-to-understand plaque now affixed to St. Enoch's. In the 1960s, with a dwindling congregation, the building was turned over to the people in the area to be used as the Don Vale Community Centre, a purpose which it fulfilled admirably until a few years ago when it was sold to the Toronto Dance Theatre, which uses it as its headquarters and for dance performances.

The building has been creatively and beautifully preserved, including the large stained glass windows, which provide St. Enoch's with much of its character.

Berkeley Street Methodist Church

At the south west corner of Queen and Berkeley, stands a very interesting looking building, apparently much older than its actual age of 113 years. The property was aquired by the church in 1857, and fourteen years later the present red brick, Gothic-style building designed by Smith and Gemmell, architects, was erected. It seated 1000 parishioners. One of the original trustees of the church was Emerson Coatsworth, later to be mayor of Toronto. An early minister in charge of Berkeley Street Methodist was Marmaduke Pearson, grandfather of Prime Minister Lester Pearson. In recent years the church has been converted to an audio-visual studio for the United Church of Canada.

All Saints' Church

Throughout its history, All Saints' Church, at the south east corner of Dundas and Sherbourne has been known for its strong sense of Christian charity, and for its non-discriminating availability to rich and poor alike. Ever since the present building was erected, in 1874, all seats are free to everyone; no pew can be sold or rented.

All Saints' was created to serve the central part of Toronto's east end, a parish carved out of that formerly belonging to Little Trinity, bounded by Carlton, Queen, Sherbourne, and the Don. However, it was expected that the church would serve primarily the recently-arrived affluent residents who lived in the substantial houses on Sherbourne Street and other streets around it, far removed, both in geography and way of life, from the Cabbagetown Irish who frequented Trinity Church. Over time the area changed, becoming less affluent and more industrialized, and many of its wealthier residents moved to Rosedale or the Annex. By the time of the Depression even the middle classes were leaving, and many of the houses once occupied only by the families of their owners, became rooming houses. By the time of the Second World War, the area had become the centre of Toronto's skid road.

As the economic make-up of its parish changed, All Saints' changed too, as its preparedness to serve rich and poor alike sustained it through periods of adversity.

The building, which seated eight hundred, was designed by Windeyer and Falloon, architects, and is in the Gothic style. It is built of white brick, with red brick decoration, a technique popular for both church and residential buildings in Toronto in the 1870s and 1880s. That it was supported at that time by persons of means is indicated by the use of a larger number of "white" bricks (the Toronto description of the light yellow bricks that resulted from the use of deeper clay, found at the brickyards of the Blue Hill on Yonge Street and in other areas around the city), which were more expensive than the red ones. The cornerstone was laid by George W. Allan, of Moss Park, one of the wealthiest men in the City. To the east of the church is a Sunday school building, of similar architectural style.

St. Bartholomew's Church

Located to-day at the south east corner of Dundas and Regent Streets, St. Bartholomew's, when it was erected in 1888-89, originally stood on the east side of River Street, at Dundas (then known as Beech Street). The parish was established in 1873 as a mission church from All Saints'. The description of St. Bart's contained in Robertson's Landmarks, states: "It is in the midst of an essentially poor neighbourhood, there being no wealthy residents or few even comparatively well to do...”[21]

In 1910, the City extended Dundas Street across the Don, so the Church had to be moved. The old building was pulled to its present site, and required extensive renovations once it stood on its new foundations. The chancel, porch and tower were built at that time, and the brick facade added to what was originally a frame roughcast building.

Church of St. Simon the Apostle

Like the congregation of St. Peter's Church, that of St. Simon's originally worshipped at the Chapel of St. James-the-Less. In the 1880s expanding population in the area indicated a need for a new Church of England parish in addition to St. Paul's and St. Peter's, which then served the area north of Cabbagetown. The present building, with half-timbering reminiscent of Elizabethan building styles, was built in 1888, to the design of architect W.L. Symons. Facing toward Howard Street, and away from Bloor Street, it provided useful service to the large residential neighbourhood which once existed where St. Jamestown now stands.

Church of the Sacred Heart (Sacré-Cœur)

In 1880, a group of French Canadians left Montreal for positions offered by a Toronto tannery. The fathers of these families, skilled leather workers, loved their work, but felt isolated in an Anglophone and Protestant-dominated environment. They were Catholics, and wanted to worship in French. To meet this need the Archbishop of Toronto asked the Archbishop of Montreal to send him a French-speaking priest. Services for the group began in the Chapel of St. Vincent De Paul in St. Michael's Palace on June 26, 1887. In September of that year, Rev. Phillippe LeMarche, a native of Monteal, was appointed pastor for the first French Canadian parish in Toronto—Sacré Cœur. A church at 430-36 King St. East was purchased at a price of twelve thousand dollars from the Presbyterians, whose congregation moved to Oak St. Its first service was held on October 7, 1888.

For three years the pastor lived at 497 King St. East, in a little lodging facing the church. Later he moved to the second storey of 493½ King St. East. After twelve years, a presbytery was built and school classes were held in the basement of the church. In 1890 there were seventy-six students listed in two classes. By 1896, the congregation had raised three thousand dollars to buy land at 58 Sackville St., and the Separate School Board erected a one storey building on the property, the first bilingual school in Toronto. After several years, another floor was added. With an increase in enroll-ment, an annex was built in the courtyard. Two hundred students, in five classes, were now in attendance. Reverend Sister Alberta was the first Director and Sister Medard the first principal.

Father LeMarche remained pastor until his death on December 21, 1924. He was known as the "Bicycle Priest" because of his custom of making his rounds on a bicycle. He devoted thirty-seven years of his life to the three to four thousand parishioners of Sacré-Cœur (thirty of those years without assistance). His nephew Fr. Edward LeMarche, came as an assistant the year before his death and succeeded him as pastor in 1924.

As the number of Francophone families grew to four hundred a site for a new church was bought at the corner of Carlton and Sherbourne Sts., at a cost of twenty thousand dollars. The corner-stone was laid on October 25, 1936 by Archbishop McGuigan. The new church building, designed by architect J. Gibb Morton is a twentieth century amalgam of a variety of medieval styles, built of brick, with dressed stone trim. It was officially opened in 1938, at which time a school building was also erected to the north. In 1950, two wings were added to the church, accommodating an additional two hundred people.

Fr. Edward LeMarche continued as pastor until his death on April 13, 1962. He was succeeded by Monsignor Alphonse Belanger who remained until his appointment as pastor at Lafontaine in 1968.

Fr. Evain Marchand assumed his duties as pastor in 1968 and held this post until June 24, 1976. Since then, Fr. Pierre Courtot has been pastor.

In ninety-four years of service Sacré-Cœur has had only five pastors, something of a record among churches.

SCHOOLS

Until the 1840s, most school classes were conducted in buildings associated with churches, or in rented premises. There was a little co-ordination of programmes and no required standards of educa-tion. The parents of children attending school were required to pay fees, which had the effect of excluding from proper education, and therefore from the possibility of self improvement, the children of Cabbagetown.

In 1844, Dr. Egerton Ryerson was appointed Superintendent of Education for Ontario, to enable him to implement the new amend-ments to the *School Act* which were based on his progressive philosophy of education. This was the birth of the Ontario public school system, which led to the abolition of fees, the offering of education to all children, the placing of responsibility for education in the hands of local elected authorities, and the standardization of educational requirements.

Pursuant to its newly-granted powers, the City of Toronto appointed its first Board of Trustees, who held their inaugural meeting in 1847. The city, however, refused to grant sufficient funds to the board to enable it to operate its schools without fees, insisting that enough be collected to cover two thirds of the cost. The board, wanting to implement the philosophy of the new Act, felt that it had no other alternative but to go out of business. Therefore every school in Toronto was closed in June 1848, and remained closed for a year.

Soon after, the province amended the Act to require municipalities to provide free schooling out of property assessments and to provide that trustees would be elected, thus freeing them from the direct control of city council. In 1851, the now-elected board decided to abolish all fees, and Park School, the first "official" free school in Toronto, opened in 1853.

There follows a brief historical description of some of the schools which educated the children of Cabbagetown:

Enoch Turner School

It may be remembered from the earlier description of Trinity Church that that institution originated from an Orangemen's march in 1842 protesting the high pew rents at St. James' Church. A second complaint voiced at the same time concerned the cost of tuition fees which virtually excluded the children of the poor Irish immigrants who lived in the Park, from access to education. Although Bishop Strachan and the businessmen who built Trinity Church were sympathetic to these legitimate concerns, there was simply no money left for a school after the church had been paid for. This was also the time, of course, in which the city was exercising its powers against providing schools which would be free to all citizens, and there was considerable public resistance in many sectors of the population to the paying of tax money for the education of other people's children.

The hero of the day was Enoch Turner (1791-1866), a local brewer whose brewery, large brick residence and spacious grounds and orchard stood just south of Front Street on the west bank of Taddle Creek, slightly north of Gooderham and Worts windmill. Enoch Turner was a popular and well-respected man. When his recently-erected brewery burned to the ground in 1832, James Worts and others of his friends arranged a loan of three hundred pounds to tide him over. He later became quite successful. Although he had no offspring of his own, he loved children, (also horses, for it was well known that he fed beer to his horses at the end of a long,

hot, thirsty day of work). His last home, Allendale, a handsome and rather unusual late Georgian-style dwelling (c. 1858), still stands to-day at 241 Sherbourne Street.

Using his own funds, Enoch Turner built a school house in 1848 on Trinity Street, just south of Little Trinity Church, the first free school in Toronto. On the day the school opened, Enoch Turner provided a full roast beef dinner with all the trimmings for the children who came to the school.

The school house was built to hold 240 children, with writing desks for 80. One master or mistress taught all classes at the school. The first master, Rev. William H. Ripley, died of cholera at the end of his first year of service, at the age of thirty-four.

The building, of simple Gothic design, built with red and white bricks similar to those used for Trinity Church, still stands to-day, and has been listed by the Toronto Historical Board as being of historical, architectural and contextual signficance. It is the oldest building in Toronto built for school purposes.

The school was taken over by the board of education, whose trustees were not pleased with the school's policy of co-education of boys and girls, or with some of its other approaches to education. When the Palace Street School was built, in 1859, it had separate rooms for pupils of each sex.

The Enoch Turner Schoolhouse continued to be used as a school until 1887, when Sackville Street School was built. It then became a Sunday school for Trinity Church. In 1971 the property was deeded to the Enoch Turner Schoolhouse Foundation, and the sum of $250,000 was raised to restore the schoolhouse, under the supervision of architect Eric Arthur. Today it is a museum and community resource, offering classes taught in the Victorian manner and dress to present-day Toronto school children.

Enoch Turner receives little mention in most of the older histories of Toronto. His story has come to light only recently, through the efforts of writers John Pope and Donald Jones.

Park School

In the early 1850s, the Toronto Board of Education recognized that the rapidly-growing population in the North Park area, (around Shuter Street) would necessitate the building of a school in that area. This led to the erection of Park School, designed by William Thomas, after a competition was held to choose the architect. Park School opened on April 5, 1853, at a site facing St. David Street, just above Shuter Street. There were separate schoolyards for boys and girls. Dr. Ryerson presided at the opening, and gave a speech.

During the first World War, a newer building was erected, this one facing south on Shuter Street, to the design of architect C.H.

A class at Park School, c. 1929,

—Jean McFarlane

Bishop. Bricks for the new school were dragged by mules up the Winchester Hill from the Don Valley brick plant. The large blocks forming its facade were hoisted into place by winches pulled by horses. Meanwhile the old building was used as a military barracks between 1914 and 1920. By 1949, Park Public School had 1,250 pupils.

Palace Street School

Situated on the east side of Cherry Street, south of Front, Palace Street School, erected in 1859, to the design of architect Joseph Sheard, is the oldest school building of the early ones established by the Toronto Board of Education. One of the early principals of the school was an exceptionally successful teacher, Georgina Riches, appointed at a time when it was unusual for a woman to be given any kind of authority in the school system. A trustee declared it would be an "outrage" for her to receive the same amount as a man's salary ($750. per year) while his wife, a teacher, earned only $250. "Perhaps that is all she is worth!" retorted Ms. Riches. Although the Trustee was able to find a technical ground upon which to fire the recalcitrant principal, a parents' petition pressured the Board into reinstating her.[22]

By 1890, the building, no longer used as a school, became part of the Cherry Street Hotel. In 1900 the hotel was enlarged as the

DUFFERIN SCHOOL

Dufferin Public School, Berkeley Street, c. 1890. The plaque at the top of the projecting portion in the centre of the building may still be seen to-day, affixed to the modern Lord Dufferin School.

—*Baldwin Room, Metropolitan Toronto Library Ref. No. T12204*

"Eastern Star" and continued in operation until the Second World War. Although in rundown condition, and hardly recognizable as what it once was, the Palace Street School may still be seen to-day. It is listed by the Toronto Historical Board.

Winchester School

In 1874, a two-room frame schoolhouse was erected west of Rose Avenue between Winchester and Prospect Streets. This was the first Winchester Public School, employing headmaster Andrew Hendry and Margaret Fraser, who taught all 207 pupils. In 1882 the school offered evening classes to adults. In 1892 a kindergarten was established.

In 1897, the present building was erected as a nine-room two-storey structure, with the third floor being added in 1901. In 1903, Winchester became one of the first two city schools to offer training in domestic science. The school has continued to serve the community around it, except for the period after a serious fire set by vandals in 1973 caused extensive damage to the building. Winchester School was restored, and to-day boasts a historical plaque erected on a stone on Winchester Street by the Toronto Historical Board.

Dufferin School (later Lord Dufferin School)

Perhaps the best known of all of the Cabbagetown schools, the Dufferin School was erected in 1876 on Berkeley Street between Gerrard and Dundas. On January 8, 1877, it opened with an enrolment of 687 pupils in an impressive three-storey large Victorian building designed by Langley, Langley and Burke, architects. In 1886 an attic storey with a mansard roof, cresting and vanes was added, creating substantial additional space and making the appearance of the school even more imposing.

At the turn of the century, Dufferin School added a commercial course, known as the "Fifth Book". Subjects offered in this course included typing, shorthand, bookkeeping, commercial law, word roots (i.e. the study of Greek and Latin roots, designed to improve spelling), history, geography and English. Previously, students wishing to continue their education had to pay to attend a collegiate or private business school, but at Dufferin there was no tuition and the books were free.

In 1925, the old Dufferin School was torn down, to be replaced with a new building. It was also re-named "Lord" Dufferin, to distinguish it from a school on Dufferin Street. To-day, the only remnant of the original building is affixed to the wall of the present one, facing Parliament Street. It is the original name and year plaque, which reads: "Dufferin City School, 1876".

Rose Avenue School

In 1883, work commenced on the construction of a four-room brick school on Rose Avenue. It opened in 1884, with 195 pupils. In 1898, Rose Avenue Home and School Association, the second oldest in the City, established an innovative "Art League" programme, to encourage pupils to grow vegetables at home in their yards. Cabbagetown had come full circle!

Sackville Street Public School

One of the most handsome school buildings in Toronto, Sackville Street Public School, at 19 Sackville Street, is one of the oldest. It was designed by architect William Storm, in "plain Victorian, style". Erected in 1887, it replaced Palace Street School and Enoch Turner School, and in 1888 had an enrolment of 269 pupils. It is Toronto's oldest building in continuous use as a school, and bears a Toronto Historical Board plaque.

CEMETERIES

As previously mentioned, the government's decision in 1795 to reserve the Park between Parliament Street and the Don for its own purposes, principally ship-building and the erection of public offices, delayed for many years the settlement of that area. It has also been described how expansion of the Town of York moved to the west, not the east or north-east as had been expected. By the 1840s, there had been very little development in the Park, and virtually no houses in the area east of Parliament and north of Gerrard (then known as Don Street). This land, far on the outskirts of the expanding city, was therefore available for large-scale uses that would be inappropriate for the downtown or residential parts of the city. The picturesque hillsides of the Don Valley north of Winchester Street and the slightly rolling land north of then Charles Street, (now Wellesley), were considered, for these reasons, well suited to provide large cemeteries.

The early history of the St. James, and Necropolis cemeteries are somewhat similar, in that each was established to replace a more central graveyard which was overcrowded, couldn't expand, and was situated in a location which rendered undesirable its continued use for the burial of the dead, since the law prohibited the establishment of further burial grounds within one mile of the city.

Chapel of St. James-the-Less, St. James' Cemetery, Parliament Street designed by Cumberland and Storm Architects, 1858.

—George H. Rust-D'Eye

St. James Cemetery

In the early days of the Town of York, the dead were buried on the grounds of St. James Church—later St. James Cathedral, on the north side of King Street between Church and Jarvis. As the town became a city and expanded around this location, it soon became clear that a new cemetery would be required. After some controversy, it was decided in 1839, that it would be established in the north-east suburbs. It was also decided to sell off some of the churchyard for commercial use, and to move the bodies of those then interred there to the new cemetery.

In 1845, sixty-five acres of land at the north end of the Park, once owned by John Graves Simcoe, were deeded to the Anglican Church of Toronto by Bishop Strachan. In that year, the grounds of the new cemetery were laid out by John G. Howard, the first city architect, who later donated High park and his house, Colborne Lodge, to the City of Toronto. Interments at St. James Cathedral ceased, and the remains of many of the earlier residents of the Town of York, together with their grave markers, were moved to the new site.

In 1858, the Chapel of St. James-the-Less was erected on a rise of ground just inside the cemetery gates. It was originally designed as simply a mortuary chapel, but in 1863 Rev. Samuel Boddy, the chaplain of the cemetery, entered on the conduct of religious services there. As the congregation expanded, it led to the creation of both St. Peter's Church, at Carlton and Bleeker Streets, and St. Simon's, north of Howard Street, after which St. James-the-Less was closed to regular worship.

The chapel, consecrated in 1861, has been called one of the ten most beautiful churches in Canada. Designed by Frederick Cumberland and William George Storm, architects, it was built in the Gothic manner of medieval churches. It stands on a high rise of ground ideally suited for it, in a setting of trees and landscaping interspersed with the sombre sculpture of the funereal craftsman. Originally there was a picket fence around the whole cemetery, but this was replaced, in 1905, by an iron fence with stone pillars, designed by architects Darling and Pearson.

If the dead could speak, the pioneers and citizens of Toronto who are buried in St. James Cemetery could tell the story of the founding of the Town of York, the structure of the Family Compact, (for most of them are here), the early administration of the Province of Upper Canada, the Government side of the Rebellion of Upper Canada, and the fight for Responsible Government. For buried on these hills, in graves marked by some of the most historic Victorian grave markers in Canada, are the following: Sir William P. Howland and James Cockburn, Fathers of Confederation; Mary Jarvis, Samuel

Grave in St. James' Cemetery of John White, Esq., Attorney-General of Upper Canada, killed in a duel with John Small, Esq., Clerk of the Executive Council, January 3rd, 1800. Mr. Small was tried for murder, and, in the custom of the day for duels, found "not guilty". Mr. White's grave was found in 1871 and his remains transported to the cemetery.
—George H. Rust-D'Eye

Gooderham and Worts family tombstones, St. James' Cemetery
George Rust-D'Eye

Peters Jarvis, and William Botsford Jarvis, of Rosedale; Chief Justices William Dummer Power, John Beverley Robinson, Sir William Meredith, Sir Glenholm Falconbridge; William Hume Blake, first chancellor of Upper Canada; architects Frederick Cumberland, William Thomas and Kivas Tulley; Rev. Henry Scadding, and John and Millicent Scadding, his parents; Enoch Turner, brewer, William George Allan, of Moss Park; Hon. Robert Baldwin Sullivan, second mayor of Toronto; William Warren Baldwin, reformer and member of the Legislative Assembly and Council, and his son Robert Baldwin, known as the founder of responsible government; Sir Casimir Gzowski, builder of the Grand Trunk Railway and prominent engineer; Thomas and William Helliwell, early Don millers; Rev. Samuel Boddy; Bishop Strachan; John White, first attorney-general of Upper Canada killed in a duel in 1800; William Gooderham; and James Worts.

In addition to the chapel, fence and gates, the following family tombs are listed by the Toronto Historical Board as being of architectural and contextual significance; Austin, Brock, Gooderham, Gzowski, Howland, Jarvis, Manning and Severs. At the entrance to the cemetery stands a sundial. Inscribed on it are the following words: "Hours fly, flowers die. New days, new ways. Pass by, love stays."

Necropolis Cemetery

The name means "city of the dead". These beautiful grounds, on the ridge of the Don Valley just north of Riverdale Park, enjoy a perfect setting. Inside the cemetery, the attractive lay-out of the grounds and the very great variety of trees and bushes, flowering shrubs and rare and exotic plants, provide an interesting and appropriate backdrop for the graves of so many of the early residents of Toronto. This was the non-sectarian, (i.e. non-Church of England) burying ground, to which were moved the graves of people who had previously been buried at Potter's Field (York General or Strangers' Burying Ground), which was situated at the north west corner of Bloor and Yonge Streets, in Yorkville. This old cemetery, established in 1825, and deriving its name from a Biblical term, (see Matthew 27:7) became surrounded by buildings, as Toronto expanded northward. It thus became considered an impediment to development, and in 1849 it was decided to open a new cemetery far to the east, in the Park.

In 1850, fifteen acres were acquired, north of the "plank road" (Winchester Street), east of Sumach; the grounds were laid out in 1858. In the 1870s the cemetery was taken over by the Trustees of the Toronto General Burying Grounds. By 1877, all of the graves had been moved to the Necropolis, and Potter's Field was closed.

Meanwhile, in 1864, the operators of the Necropolis bought several acres of land south of Winchester Street to provide for expansion of the cemetery. However, after protests by residents of the community, the city had to step in and purchase the land, which later became part of Riverdale Park.

In 1872, the beautiful chapel, gate and gatehouse were erected, to the designs of architect Henry Langley, a perfect entrance to the attractive terraces and picturesque walkways which characterize the Necropolis. The grounds were originally surrounded by a neat Gothic picket fence. In the grounds is a handsome mausoleum, a vault intended for the reception of the dead and storage during the winter months while the ground was too hard to allow burials. Later, in 1933, a well-designed crematorium, by architect J.F. Brown, was erected.

Like St. James Cemetery, the Necropolis is the resting place of many of Toronto's pioneers. A special marker and plaque stand near the west end of the grounds commemorating the early Torontonians whose remains are buried here.

Also near the east fence on Sumach Street is the grave of Samuel Lount and Peter Matthews who, in April 1838, were executed by hanging at the public square on King Street, for their part in the Rebellion of Upper Canada. In the 1850's their leader in the rebellion, William Lyon Mackenzie, together with three relatives of Samuel Lount, moved the bodies to the Necropolis. In 1893 a public subscription raised money to build a suitable memorial to the rebels, resulting in the erection of the present large granite memorial bearing a broken column, symbolizing the lives that had been cut short. Printed in the stone is the story of the two unfortunate rebels. Behind this monument stands the original small stone marker bearing simply the names Samuel Lount and Peter Matthews, and the words "both buried in one grave".

William Lyon Mackenzie himself is buried in the Necropolis, on a high spot toward the east end of the grounds, his grave marked by a large Gaelic cross. Also lying in the Necropolis are George Brown, a Father of Confederation and founder of the Toronto *Globe*; Ned Hanlan, rowing champion and alderman of Toronto; John Ross Robertson, writer, philanthropist and founder of the *Evening Telegram*; William Howland, mayor of Toronto 1886-87; Sir John Alexander Boyd, last chancellor of Ontario; and Peter Rothwell Lamb, proprietor of the local glue and blacking factory and father of Daniel Lamb, founder of the Riverdale Zoo.

When the old-timers of Cabbagetown were young, the Necropolis was considered an excellent playground. Although over the years many of the grave markers have deteriorated, nevertheless most are still readable. In any event, the Necropolis is a beautiful place to visit, a walking tour all of its own, as is its neighbour, St. James Cemetery to the north. Members of the public are always welcome.

THE TORONTO GENERAL HOSPITAL AND RELATED INSTITUTIONS

The first general hospital in Toronto was built in 1817 at the corner of King and John Streets. It remained in operation for thirty-nine years, except for a five-year period commencing 1829, when the government took over the building, after the previous buildings of government had burned down. In 1833, when legislation first provided for the establishment of local boards of health, pressures grew for the building of a new hospital beyond the city limits.

In 1854, the newly-appointed trustees of the Toronto General Hospital decided to build the hospital in the Park Reserve. This decision was not made without controversy. The miasma thought to be exuded from the marshes and swamps around the Don had given the area a very bad name, since it was well-known throughout the city that residents of that area suffered from fever and the ague. The problems of health pointed to by the critics certainly existed, but many of them were caused by the insufficient housing and unsanitary living conditions in which these people had to live. Cows and pigs roamed the streets; garbage collection was sporadic.

It was pointed out by one of the supporters of the new hospital, that all of the refuse and waste from the city ended up in the bay, from which "the delicious mixture of feculent matter and bay water is served up through pipes and distributed throughout the city to be swallowed by citizens." The proposed site for the new hospital, on the other hand, was eighty feet above Lake Ontario, distant from the unhealthy city, and with a good water supply of its own.

In 1854, tenders were received, and in 1856 the new building, on the north side of Gerrard between Sackville and Sumach, opened to receive its first patients. It had accommodation for 250 patients, and a medical staff of eight, with four consulting doctors on call. The hospital building, designed by William Hay, architect, was a huge four-storey "castle" with five imposing towers along its 170-foot facade. The central tower was 100 feet high. Both it and the rest of the building were surmounted by a high mansard roof. It was a stately building, of white brick with stone dressings, designed in the fifteenth century English domestic style. As the years went by, it became almost totally covered with ivy.

Its wards were large, with four bathrooms per floor; two with toilets. Each ward could hold from eight to twelve patients. The wards were roomy and well-ventilated. There was a water hydrant in every corridor, and ventilation facilities for the drawing away of foul air. In each ward was a ventilator flue to draw impure vapour into the open air.

Associated with the hospital were: a fever hospital; the Mercer eye and ear infirmary, with forty beds; a dispensary for women; the Burnside lying-in hospital for maternity cases, with thirty beds; a resort for convalescent patients; a mortuary; and, by 1881, a school of nursing, only the second in Canada. The operating theatre was in the centre of the building. The complex occupied four acres, the grounds of which were surrounded by a high picket fence.

The hospital developed an excellent reputation, and was used for teaching medical students of three universities and three medical schools. One minor setback occurred in 1867, when, because of financial difficulties, the hospital had to close for a year. Additions were made to the building in 1877, 1878, 1880, 1882 and 1888.

In 1914, the new Toronto General Hospital on College Street opened, and the old one on Gerrard was virtually abandoned, although immediately after the First World War, regiments of the 48th Highlanders and the Queen's Own Rifles were quartered in the hospital building. Neighbours would awaken to the sound of bugles and the tramping of marching feet.

In 1922, the building was torn down, and replaced by rows of small, new houses on Sumach, Gifford, Nasmith and Sackville. It is said that the residents of these new houses tended to look down upon their surrounding neighbours who lived in old houses.

A Toronto Historical Board plaque on the north side of Spruce Street bears a short history of the great hospital which once stood across the street.

Ontario Medical College for Women

At 289 Sumach Street stands a building, erected in 1890, which once housed the foremost medical school for women in Canada, the forerunner of Women's College Hospital. The School was established in 1883 by Dr. Michael Barrett at the urging of the Women's Suffrage Club of Toronto, at a time when other Toronto medical schools would not admit women. It began in a rented cottage on Sumach, and then opened its new building in 1890, equipped with the best medical aparatus of the day. In 1891, it was staffed by six lecturers and demonstrators, including Dr. Augusta Stowe Cullen, the first woman to get a medical degree from an Ontario university, and daughter of Dr. Emily Howard Jennings Stowe, the first female medical practitioner in Canada. Another staff member who attracted great interest in the community, was Dr. Jennie Gray, who would drive up to the college in her horseless carriage.

Associated with the medical school was the Women's Dispensary, started in 1896 by Anna McFee, a medical student, in a house on St. David Street, in which women physicians could treat their own patients. The clinic proved very popular, soon moving to the medical

Toronto General Hospital, (1856-1913)
Photograph   186-   by W. Notman, one side of a stereopticon card
—Baldwin Room, Metropolitan Public Library, Ref. No. T 30148

A busy day at the Women's Dispensary, 18 Seaton Street, in 1914.

—*City of Toronto Archives Ref: Health Dept. 339*

Trinity Medical School 41 Spruce Street c. 1900   — *Trinity College*

school. When the school merged with the medical faculty of the University of Toronto, in 1903, the dispensary continued on its own in a building at Parliament and Queen, then moved, in 1910, to 18 Seaton Street, and later to 125 Rusholme Road, where it had facilities to handle fifty adult patients and twenty-five babies. After it had moved from 18 Seaton Street, that house became a home for unwed mothers.

Trinity College Medical School

The building at 41 Spruce Street, now part of a housing develop-ment, was built in 1871 as the Trinity College Medical School. A controversy among doctors over teaching methods led to the crea-tion of three medical schools, one of which was Trinity. The first Dean of the School was Dr. E.M. Hodder, a surgeon and yachtsman, one of the founders of modern medicine in Canada, and one of the first doctors to advocate the use of more efficient antiseptics. He was also a great obstetrician and gynaecologist, and during his career delivered seven thousand babies.

The college was incorporated as an independent medical school, but in 1887 affiliated with Toronto Medical College. The building contained a semi-circular lecture hall, a reading room, and a library; in the rear was a one-storey building used as a dissecting room. From time to time the floors of that room were waxed and used by the students for dancing. In the basement was a modern laboratory.

Gordon Sinclair tells the story, confirmed by others, how on one Halloween night, students slipped out of the medical school carrying a long bundle all wrapped in cloth. The next morning, early shoppers were shocked to see that among the deer and pigs suspended by meat hooks outside Silk's butcher shop on Parliament Street was the naked body of a man. Policemen began to unravel the mystery when they noticed that the lifeless form gave off an unmistakeable odour of formaldahyde. Soon after, both the cadaver and some students found themselves in a pickle!

In 1903 the college federated with the University of Toronto and moved to that campus. The building was purchased by the Sleepmaster Mattress Company, which used it as a warehouse until the early 1970s. In 1979 the building was cleaned and converted into four dwelling units. To-day it boasts a Toronto Historical Board plaque.

The Toronto School of Medicine

The Toronto School of Medicine, one of the others resulting from dissension among doctors, stood at the south west corner of Sack-ville and Gerrard. It became the medical faculty of Victoria College, and was later demolished for the Regent Park development.

THE CONSUMERS GAS COMPANY

On December 28, 1841, the first gas lights were lit in Toronto, supplied by a firm which was to become the City of Toronto Gas, Light and Water Company, incorporated in 1842, whose works were at the foot of Princess Street. Before then, lighting was provided by tallow candles. In 1846, the court house was the first public building to be illuminated by gas.

In 1847, a meeting of gas light consumers resolved to form a company to be called the Consumers' Gas Company. In 1848 the company was incorporated, purchased the City of Toronto Gas, Light, and Water Company, and began to supply gas to the city. The contract with customers stipulated "lighting must not commence on any day before the sun has set, and all lights must be extinguished each night within 10 minutes after the hour contracted for."

In 1855, the company erected new works on a three-acre site on the east side of Parliament near the bay, just north of the present Mill Street.

In 1860, gas lights were used to illuminate a series of triumphal

Toronto General Hospital, Gerrard Street

—Artwork on Toronto, 1898

arches and the outlines of prominent buildings at the time of the visit of the Prince of Wales. Gas lights were also used to light the St. Lawrence Hall in 1851, when P.T. Barnum brought his star, Jenny Lind, to sing for a charity event. By 1873, the company served 2,050 customers, and had installed 740 street lamps.

Coal from Pennsylvania to be used for the production of gas, was shipped across Lake Ontario and unloaded at a wharf at Esplanade and Berkeley Streets. Later it came in by rail.

During the period 1883 to 1890, the Consumers' Gas Co. embarked on a major extension of its works, building large new brick buildings on the west side of Berkeley, south of Front, almost filling the blocks between Berkeley and Trinity streets including the site of the first parliament buildings, and on the north east corner of Parliament and Front. Altogether, the gasworks extended over ten acres. Of the buildings and gasometers built during this period, comprising the Company's Station A, only four structures remain. These include the pump room, which became the Toronto Free Theatre, and the engine house and another pump room, which became the headquarters of Greenspoon Wreckers, who were hired to wreck the building and instead fell in love with it and decided to keep it. An interesting story about the Toronto Free Theatre building, provided by the ROMwalk people, is that while the building was being renovated, a five hundred thousand gallon tank full of sulphuric acid was found imbedded in the floor of the main area of the building, and had to be pumped out.

A third building, a purifying house, at the south west corner of Front and Berkeley, was recently in use by Dalton's Cherries (1834) Limited, a firm which started business in London in 1834, and moved to Toronto in 1873. It has recently been acquired by the Canadian Opera Company.

All of these buildings were erected in 1887 to the designs of Strickland and Symonds, architects. Interesting examples of late Victorian industrial architecture, they include Romanesque and Queen Anne elements.

The other building of the complex which remains is the large purifying house at the north east corner of Front and Parliament. When it was built, in 1899, and extended in 1904, it replaced a large cluster of working class housing that backed onto the Copland's Brewery complex at Parliament and Derby. It was designed by Bond and Smith, architects.

THE POLICE

In 1877, J. Timperlake wrote:

> The police force of Toronto is probably the finest, best drilled, most effective, and most intelligent civic police force on the American continent.

It seems that most Cabbagetowners would have agreed with that statement, for most people who lived there got along with the police, and vice versa. Of course, part of this may have had to do with the fact that so many police officers were Irishmen. Residents would often call policemen "uncle", and everyone knew the local cop on the beat. Policemen in those days wore the old "bobby" helmets, and rode bicycles, except for inspectors, who drove Model A Fords.

One of the most popular policemen ever to work in Toronto was Detective Jimmy Ledlie, who in 1958 retired after thirty years in the Force. Citizens and other police officers jammed Columbus Hall, on Sherbourne Street, to pay tribute to "the kindliest guy that ever put on a uniform". Jimmy Ledlie's philosophy was that as a policeman you meet a lot of people in trouble, and your job is to get them out of trouble, not into more. This policy was put into practice on many occasions, such as the many times when he would buy a ticket to send a boy home rather than arrest him. Often, he would speak in court in favour of those he had arrested, even those with long records. He worked long hours, but the smile never left his face.

THE FIRE DEPARTMENT

Until 1874, fire protection was provided by volunteers under civic control. Before 1861, the men pulled their engines to fires. In that year the first horse-drawn pumpers were acquired, and the horses learned to run from their stables at the sound of an alarm and up to the front door of the station, where their harness would be hanging ready to drop over them before they went racing to the fire. In 1874, the Toronto Fire Department was established, with paid firemen. In 1916, the first motorized fire trucks were brought in, and in 1921, the last steamer was taken out of service.

The fire stations which served Cabbagetown were Deluge No. 5, Berkeley Street, west side north of King later replaced by No. 4

Number 4 Fire Station, west side of Berkeley north of King Street East, 186___. This station, built in 1859, was later, in 1885 replaced by a new fire hall. Its successor, built in 1905, is now the Firehall Theatre.

—Province of Ontario Archives Ref. No. S14180

Members of the first shift at No. 7 fire station, Dundas St. East at Parliament, 1922
—*History of the Toronto Fire Department, Published by the Burial Fund of the Toronto Fire Fighters, 1922.*

Members of the second shift at No. 4 fire station, Berkeley St., 1922
—*History of the Toronto Fire Department, Published by the Burial Fund of the Toronto Fire Fighters, 1922*

Station, (1859) in turn replaced in 1885; Wilton Avenue, No. 7, north east corner of Dundas and Parliament (1878); joined with No. 4 police station, it had a very high hose drying tower, and carved heads of a fireman and a policeman respectively in keystones over the doors to the stations, (demolished in the 1950s); No. 11 Station at Rose Avenue and Howard Streets, (demolished).

ALLAN GARDENS

One of the early settlers of the Town of York was William Allan, who came here in 1796: In 1819 he bought the one hundred acre Park Lot between Sherbourne and Jarvis Streets, where in 1830 he built his mansion, a house named Moss Park, between Shuter and Queen Streets. After his death in 1853, his son, George William Allan, president of the Horticultural Society of Toronto, (also later to be mayor of Toronto and president of the Senate) decided to donate land to the city to be used for horticultural gardens so that his fellow citizens could share with him his lifelong love of flowers. This grant of five acres of land was made in 1857. He also leased an additional five acres to the City for a nominal rent.

On September 11, 1860 the park was formally opened by the Prince of Wales, who planted a young maple tree there. In 1878, a "crystal palace" pavilion was built. For some years the property was under control of the Horticultural Society, but in 1888 it came back to the city, and ever since has been a city park. In 1885 the grounds were beautifully laid out, with lawns, flower beds and seats. The largest and finest fountain in Ontario stood near the centre of the grounds, the site of the present very puny memorial to Toronto historian G. Mercer Adam. The park was named Allan Gardens in 1901, the year that George W. Allan died.

In June 6, 1902, a fire destroyed the old pavilion, which had been the only large concert hall in use in Toronto for most of the previous twenty years. In 1909, the present Palm House, designed by architect R. McCallum, was built in its place. An addition was built to it in 1913. It contains a choice collection of native and foreign plants, rare orchids and other exotic plants, and, of course, palms.

Although Allan Gardens is not in Cabbagetown, its association with the people of that area is so close that it is fair to include it as part of Cabbagetown life.

Most of the action in Juan Butler's novel, *Cabbagetown Diary,*[23] takes place in either Moss Park or Allan Gardens.

In front of the Palm House stands a provincial historical plaque commemorating the Toronto Horticultural Society.

The pavilion and fountain, Horticultural Gardens (later Allan Gardens)

—Artwork on Toronto, 1898

The polar bear gets a drink, Riverdale Zoo, 1923.

—City of Toronto Archives

A Saturday crowd, Riverdale Zoo, 1913.

RIVERDALE PARK, ZOO AND FARM

In 1856, the City of Toronto purchased 119 acres from the Scadding estate for the purposes of a park and industrial farm (jail with surrounding lands for prisoners to work). On August 11, 1880, Riverdale Park was officially opened. In 1890, all of the lands except the jail property were designated to remain in park use. Including other additions made since, Riverdale Park consists of about 162 acres, much of it built on garbage and manure landfill laid out by prisoners from the jail.

In 1894, the gift to Toronto of two wolves and a few deer became the first acquisition of what was to be an outstanding zoological collection. Most of these animals, and the zoo which was built to house them, were obtained through the efforts of Daniel Lamb, a

city Alderman, who lived nearby, at 156 Winchester Street, and who best deserves the title "father of the Riverdale Zoo."

It appears that the first exhibition of animals at Riverdale Zoo took place in 1899. The collection grew quickly, as Alderman Lamb encouraged prominent people to donate animals or money to buy animals. By 1902, the zoo had acquired sixteen pheasants, two ocelots, a male camel, a female dromedary, a buffalo bull, six pens of monkeys, a Siberian bear, a young female crane, some lions and a hippo. The first weekend that the elephant and lions were shown, the Toronto Railway Company carried twenty thousand people to the zoo.

Eva Broomhall remembers that the grounds around the zoo provided a wonderful playground for kids, with flower beds, benches and lots of green grass. The grounds were cared for by prisoners from the Don Jail, men who had committed minor crimes, such as

At the Riverdale Zoo, c. 1900. In the background is the 'Donnybrook', built in 1902 and still standing, vacant, in 1984

—From a Postcard

vagrancy. Many were befriended by visitors to the zoo. Some of the children also were quite friendly with the zoo keepers, and often went with them when they fed the animals.

In 1902 the Toronto Railway Company arranged for the erection of a two-storey building of Moorish design, built of stone and pressed brick with a tile roof, a fanciful little edifice which, apart from the zookeepers's cottage and a small wildfowl pavilion, is the only building from the original zoo still standing to-day. It was named the Donnybrook. An interesting fact about the Donnybrook, provided to us by former Alderman Janet Howard, is that soon after the cement basement floor of the Donnybrook had been poured, but before it had dried, a hippo, no doubt looking for a quiet and shady place to relax, and spying what appeared to be a large mud puddle in the floor, sat down, leaving there, as a monument to the early days of the Riverdale Zoo, a perfect hippo bottom print!

At sunset on June 30, 1974, the Riverdale Zoo closed its gates for the last time, and its animals were shipped up to the new Metro Zoo. Most of the buildings were torn down, except for the Donnybrook and the original stone gate posts at Winchester and Sumach, which used to anchor a fence that ran around the park. They had lanterns on top when they were first built. Soon after the zoo closed, plans were made to develop the site into a Victorian animal farm.

A large ninety by fifty-foot Pennsylvania German-style bank barn, built in the 1850's, was donated by the Francy Family of Markham, and moved here in pieces and reconstructed by Campbell and Gary Snider. The structure of this barn is original, including pieces of white pine twelve by fourteen inches and fifty feet long. The barn, which has an unusual overhang on its south side, was originally constructed by a Tunker community of Pennsylvania Germans, under the direction of Richard Lewis.

The other two buildings on the site are new, although the farm house is built of reclaimed brick. Both that house, which is a replica of the type of 1850s Ontario farm house found on the Francy farm, and the barn, were designed by architect B. Napier Simpson Jr., a nationally-renowned expert in building conservation and restoration, long-time member of the Toronto Historical Board, and member of the National Sites and Monuments Board. While working for the latter board, he was killed in an airplane crash in Newfoundland in 1978. In memory of its architect, the house has been named the Napier Simpson Farmhouse, and is marked by a Toronto Historical Board plaque unveiled by his son. The house, being a 1970s building, is also the newest entry on the Toronto Historical Board inventory. It is also one of only two major replica buildings in the city, the other being the Bellevue Fire Hall.

The Riverdale Farm has quickly become a much loved feature of the Don Vale community, especially among its younger members. Although admission is always free, and it is a resource belonging to all of Toronto, it is never crowded, except when busloads of school children come in to see it. An ideal employment of the site, the farm blends in beautifully with the pleasant setting and picturesque Victorian buildings of the Necropolis across Winchester Street.

STRAIGHTENING OF THE DON

The Don River once meandered lazily through its valley, and was the scene of pleasant boat-rides, picnicking, fishing, hiking and all of the other bucolic pastimes that a clean natural river can provide. In 1881, however, there began to emerge a plan to straighten and deepen the Don, ostensibly to remove impediments to transportation, and cure the unhealthy conditions which its marshes were thought to produce. Charles Sauriol, in his recently-published book *Remembering the Don*,[24] suggests that: "The straightening of the Don was...considered necessary to provide land primarily for industrial purposes and to also make available an additional railway entrance to Toronto. The Don with a greater depth of water after improvement could also be used to convey shipping up to the Queen Street station."

A private company formed to promote the project, wanted to be given the power to expropriate, so that they could take possession of waste riparian land, reclaim it, and lease it to industrial concerns. They appeared before City Council with this scheme, arguing that if the Don were staightened, the water would be purified, and fever and ague banished. The City decided instead to seek a mandate from its constituency to carry out the project itself.

In 1886, the people of Toronto voted "to improve and straighten the River Don so as to secure the sanitary condition of that part of the City of Toronto contiguous to the said river."

The work that was then commenced included the removal of five small islands between Queen and Winchester Streets, and the straightening of three big meanders and two small ones. Excavation and dredging resulted in the cutting of a channel from Winchester Street to the lake. Huge thirty foot-long ten inch cedar piles were hammered in along the new "banks" of the river, while fill taken from the hillsides surrounding the Don Valley permanently altered the appearance of the landscape. The marshes and swamps which had existed for centuries around the Don and at Ashbridges Bay, disappeared forever.

Strangely enough, the original plans, to bring vessels up to Gerrard Street, to build wharf accommodation along the banks of the Don, and to provide swing bridges for the unobstructed passage of ships, were never carried through. However, for a while there was some shipping activity on the Don up to Winchester, by the ferry *Minnie Kidd* and the steam barges *Gordon Jerry, May Bird* and *Honey Dew.*

Meanwhile, a squabble developed between the two principal beneficiaries of the plan. Grand Trunk Railway and Canadian Pacific Railway, over the right-of-way over the newly-formed access to Toronto. Eventually litigation ended up with C.P.R. getting the east side and G.T.R. the west.

Thus, the foregoing "improvements", together with the increasing amount of pollutants poured into the Don by the many industries operating on its banks, turned a natural and peaceful river valley into a large open sewer guarded on each side by an impassible ribbon of steel.

Until the last few years, the Don River, not wanting to acknowledge that it had been straightened, gained some small degree of revenge each spring, when run-offs and rain would cause all of the baseball diamonds on the created flatland at the foot of the hill at Carlton Street to flood and turn into a sea of mud; for, this little indentation into the hillsides of the Don Valley, was once the river's bed.

THE BELT LINE RAILWAY

In 1890 someone thought it would be a great idea to develop a commuter train line to loop into the developing suburbs of Toronto, and provide a comfortable and scenic trip for those who lived in, and those who wanted to buy, new houses in those areas in which real estate speculation was just beginning to have its effects. The idea was attributed to Henry W. Tyler, president of the Grand Trunk Railway, but implemented by a private Belt Line Company.

By 1891, the tracks were completed, with loops through the Don and Humber valleys respectively, linked by a line across the waterfront and an east-west section starting just above the Mount Pleasant Cemetery. The Belt Line opened for business on July 30, 1892, using tracks leased from the G.T.R. The company had two engines and five coaches, with facilities for carrying freight. Trains ran six times daily in each direction, taking one hour and ten minutes to complete the whole route. The fare was fairly high, at twenty-five cents a trip or five cents per station. The stations on the Don Valley loop were Moore Park, Rosedale, Don Valley, Gerrard, Don and Union Station.

The scheme was an unqualified failure. The high fares, the decline in suburban real estate sales, and generally a lack of demand for service of this kind, resulted in few people using the Belt Line. It was an idea ahead of its time. In six months the bankrupt company was taken over by the Grand Trunk Railway, which operated the Belt Line until November 17, 1894, when the line was closed.

The Belt Line Railway is not to be confused with the very popular Belt Line streetcar loop-line. Although the former line offered a spectacular scenic ride for its few patrons, and its existence did have the effect of inflating land values, nevertheless the Belt Line had little lasting impact on Toronto, other than to leave available for public use a cleared swath of trail through picturesque parts of the Don Valley and some areas around the Mount Pleasant Cemetery and Chaplin Crescent, parts of which are now public parkland.

STREET CARS

In 1861 the first exclusive franchise to operate a street railway system was granted to the Toronto Street Railway Company. The horse-drawn trams were to run no more than thirty minutes apart, at

The Prince Edward Viaduct, shown c. 1930

—View Album of Toronto, Valentine-Black Co. Ltd.

speeds no more than six miles per hour, for sixteen hours a day in summer and fourteen hours in winter. There were no transfers and the fare on each route was five cents. During the term of its thirty-year franchise, the T.S.R.C. laid down sixty-eight miles of track. By 1891, when its operating rights expired, it owned 361 vehicles,100 sleighs, 1,372 horses, and was carrying fifty-five thousand passengers a day.[25]

In 1891, the city briefly took over ownership of the railway, but then granted a new thirty-year franchise to the newly-formed Toronto Railway Company. In 1884 the first successful electric railway in North America had been established at the Exhibition Grounds, and by 1892, the T.R.C. began to use electric cars on its lines. On August 31, 1894, the last horse car was withdrawn from service. Fares for the T.R.C. were five cents cash, six for twenty-five cents or twenty-five for one dollar, and transfer privileges were allowed.

During the period 1891-97 there was a great public controversy over Sunday street cars, which were finally allowed, by popular vote, in 1897. On September 1, 1921, the street railway system was taken over by the Toronto Transportation Commission, which, in 1954, became the Toronto Transit Commission.

The first streetcars operating in Cabbagetown were Toronto Street Railway vehicles, which ran on King; Queen; Carlton, (east to Parliament); Gerrard, (west to Parliament); Winchester (Sumach to Parliament); Parliament, (Queen to Winchester); and Sherbourne. When a horse car reached the end of its route, for instance at Winchester and Sumach, the horse would simply be unhitched and moved around to the other end of the car before starting back on its single-track route. The seats, too, could be turned around by flipping up the back. There were no window panes in these cars, and the driver was seated in the open. They were very slow. The car would stop when a passenger rang the bell.

Most of the above horse-tram lines were continued under the Toronto Railway Company, but, as mentioned, electric cars were in operation after the early 1890s. These cars had window panes, and were heated.

Cabbagetown old-timers remember that people with baby carriages used to hook them on the back of street cars as they got on; sometimes a car would have up to four or five carriages, hanging to it as it rolled along. Until the 1920s, some open air cars were still in operation, with the conductor walking up and down the sides to collect the fares.

ROADS AND TRAFFIC

The Town of York was known as "Muddy York" from its earliest days to well into the nineteenth century. By 1834, when York became the City of Toronto, there was some road "paving" in the form of macadam, which was often little better than gravel spread over hard-packed dirt. At this time there were plank sidewalks in areas of the "downtown", consisting of two twelve-inch planks laid side by side.

By 1860, the paving had improved somewhat. The Toronto Street Railway Company, in laying its track, began to use six-inch-deep cedar blocks to pave the trackbeds. This technique proved popular, and by the 1870s the City began to install cedar block paving on many of its streets. By the 1880s, many of the major streets in Cabbagetown were paved with cedar block. The last cedar block throughfare in Toronto, a laneway between Pembroke and George streets just north of Dundas, was torn up in 1976.

In the 1880s, cobblestones were used on some roads, sometimes to replace cedar blocks that had been dug out by citizens for use as firewood. The cobblestones, were durable, and wouldn't burn, but like the cedar blocks, they tended to get very slippery when wet.

In the 1890s, brick paving was introduced. The end of Carlton Street east of Sumach, still has its original brick paving, one of a decreasing number of brick-paved streets left in the city. Although Portland cement was first manufactured in 1824, it was not used for paving in Toronto until well into the 1880s and 1890s, when the techniques used to make six-inch "granolithic" concrete sidewalks were applied to road-making as well.

The first street in Toronto laid with asphalt was Bay Street, in 1888, and gradually other roads throughout the city were similarly improved, just in time to greet the arrival of the motor car.

Originally considered a novelty, costing up to five thousand dollars each, automobiles quickly became popular as prices decreased, and they began to replace horses. Soon trucks began to appear, and many of the businesses started using them for deliveries, although there were still horse-drawn delivery vans and junk wagons in Toronto in the late 1940s. The motor car was considered a novelty for at least the first decade of this century. In 1909, the Supreme Court of Ontario found that it was actionable negligence to park a shiny red car with brass lamps and fittings by the side of the road, because it might scare passing horses.[26]

In the vicinity of Cabbagetown, Hupmobiles were assembled north of the Sunlight Soap works on the other side of the Don. William

Hambly remembers that his great uncle, Samuel Rogers (whose brother, Elias, was a fuel dealer), started off delivering coal, throwing away gasoline as a useless commodity. Soon, however, he realized what a market there was for this product, and so founded the Queen City Oil Company, now Imperial Oil.

In the early days, gasoline was available from hardware stores. In Cabbagetown, the first gasoline pumps stood outside Nettleship's Hardware on Parliament Street, near Wellesley.

THE DON JAIL

Although not within the boundaries of Cabbagetown, the nearby Don Jail was certainly a fixture in the life of some Cabbagetowners, and fondly remembered by old-timers who, as children, played in the area and watched the police load and unload the Black Maria with its human cargo. It is also a great architectural work by William Thomas, one of Toronto's most important architects, who also designed, among other buildings, the St. Lawrence Hall and St. Michael's Cathedral.

Work on the fourth Toronto Jail, which was to replace the one on the site of the old Parliament Buildings at the foot of Berkeley Street, was begun in 1859. On October 24, 1859, a procession from the City Hall on Front Street, to the Industrial Farm, on Gerrard, the site of the new jail, was followed by a cornerstone-laying ceremony, after which a luncheon was held at which wine flowed freely. The more-than-slightly-inebriated officials rounded out the day by singing "For He's a Jolly Good Fellow" to the tune of "God Save the Queen".

By January 17, 1862, the jail was almost completed when, at 2:00 A.M., the building caught fire. The caretaker, awakened by the fire, ran through deep snow to Berkeley Street, where he put in a fire alarm from the box, and returned to do what he could to fight the conflagration. However, when the fire engines arrived at Berkeley Street, the firemen saw no fire, and so returned to their station. A later alarm was given, but because of the deep snow, firefighters did not arrive until 5:00 A.M. Then they discovered there wasn't enough hose to reach to the jail from the Don River, and it wasn't until 7:00 A.M. that sufficient hose was brought to the scene. By 1:00 P.M. in the afternoon, the building was gutted. This is a useful story for Cabbagetowners to consider while the fast and efficient No. 7 trucks of to-day roar past their windows at two in the morning.

The Don Jail was re-built and opened its doors to its first visitors in 1865. Professor Eric Arthur describes the Don Jail as "a friendly building in spite of its rustications, vermiculated quoins and barred

Keystone over the door, Don Jail, William Thomas, Architect, (1858)
—George Rust-D'Eye

Parliament Street looking north from Queen Street, 1917

—City of Toronto Archives, Salmon   E 1467

The Don Jail, Gerrard Street, 1870's

—*Province of Ontario Archives*

windows."[27] Its architecture is said to have been inspired by classical Italian and English Renaissance forms. Its white brick central block is formal, befitting the dignity of a major public building. Over the central doorway is a magnificent carved keystone of a man's face, with flowing beard and hair, welcoming all who enter. Flanking the central pavilion are two buff-coloured brick wings.

Inside is a setting of spaciousness and grandeur, with a skylighted eighty foot-high tower, ringed by a double row of carefully detailed cast iron balconies, held up by brackets bearing the iron likenesses of dragons and serpents. The Don Jail, with its uplifting interior and well lighted and ventilated cells, reflected the humanitarian principles of rehabilitative justice which the erection of such a magnificent building for this purpose was intended to embody.

Built to house three hundred prisoners in a relatively attractive environment, the jail later suffered an undeserved bad reputation, caused not by its own inadequacies but from the ways in which it was used. By the time it finally ceased to be used as a jail, in the late 1970s, it housed six hundred prisoners, twice as many as it was intended to accommodate. It now sits vacant, awaiting, it is hoped, cleaning and restoration, and the finding of an appropriate and sympathetic use.

A view through Spruce Court, an excellent low-dividend housing project, on Spruce Street, to the towers of the Toronto General Hospital (1856—1913), shown in c. 1920.

—City of Toronto Archives Ref: James Collection 3106

SPRUCE COURT

The Spruce Court housing development constructed by the Toronto Housing Company in the period 1913 to 1926, represents the first successful application of the limited dividend housing concept in Canada. The philosophy behind Spruce Court, and its sister project on Bain Avenue on the east side of the Don, was to utilize public guarantees of private non-profit development for the purpose of providing good low-rental accommodation to working class wage earners. It involved a combination of public and private initiative, and encouraged as well the voluntary cooperation of citizens, who would also become involved in the administration of the project.

Profits which resulted after repayment of private capital would enure to the benefit of those co-operating in the venture.

Aside from the economic aspects of the project, the planning considerations and housing design were also unusually far-sighted for the day, based on the English "garden city" ideal. This approach involved an attempt to combine the best characteristics of city and country life, and bring people in contact with the land in comfortable small houses in an attractive setting.

Purchasing property in the suburbs, (Spruce and Sumach Streets), in anticipation of further extension of the Toronto Railway Company lines, the Toronto Housing Company hired one of the foremost architects of the day, Eden Smith, to design the "cottage flats" for Spruce Court. This choice was a good one, for what resulted was a pleasing and well-planned series of dwelling units, built in rows fairly

97

close to the road on one side, but each one opening out on a large central court, or garden, on the other. Each unit had its own address (1-60 Gildersleeve Place), and unit number, and a covered verandah, or sun porch, overlooking the common areas.

The houses boasted many other features, including central heating for the whole development and hot water available throughout the year; each unit had its own bathroom, sink, laundry tub and gas stove. The design of the homes was graceful, dignified and functional. The houses were planned for durability, with an expected life span of forty to fifty years. Now, seventy years later, they are still providing comfortable accommodation to their residents.

However, the project was not considered an unqualified success, because although the homes were well designed, the rents were beyond the reach of those for whom they were intended. The rents averaged over twenty-five dollars per month, half of the average salary of those aimed at, and although that sum included hot water, city water, repairs, maintenance, snow clearance, lawn upkeep and taxes, it was still felt that rents of this level were no better than those offered by the private sector.

Delayed by the depression of 1913, the project was completed in 1926 by the architectural firm of Mathers and Haldenby.

GIRL'S HOME

On the south side of Gerrard Street, between Ontario and Seaton Streets, just below the Brewers' Retail parking lot, stands an old building, now a union hall, which was once dedicated "to the rescue and care of young girls and the bestowal of careful attention to their religious, moral and temporal welfare".[28] The Girls' Home, later Protestant Girls' Home, was built in 1871-72. Originally established as a nursery school, the previous building was enlarged in 1860 to admit girls up to fifteen years of age and train them for household work. During the Depression, it served as a men's hostel, and appears since that time to have been moved somewhat southward from its original site.

CENTRAL NEIGHBOURHOOD HOUSE

On September 18, 1911, Central Neighbourhood House opened its doors for the first time, as "a democratic meeting place for people of all races, creeds, cultures and ages", a social centre for the neighbourhood, a "headquarters for sane and sympathetic observations of the conditions and needs in the district", and "a centre for testing and developing methods of social services." These were its goals, as stated by the Victoria College students who, with some interested citizens, established Central Neighbourhood House.

Over the seventy-one years of its existence it has served these goals well. Its first "house" was in the Ward, at 84 Gerrard Street West. Since that time it has moved from place to place, and finally to its present location, at 349 Ontario Street.

DIXON HALL

Dixon Hall, a "neighbourhood social and family service centre," was opened in 1929 on Sumach Street through the efforts of Canon Dixon, of Little Trinity Chruch, and Rev. William Edgar Wilson, who worked for thirty-five years in the Moss Park district. In the early days of the Depression the Hall operated a soup kitchen which served five hundred portions of soup and bread daily. The sick and the elderly, the poor and the helpless, were visited at home and helped in every way possible. Throughout the years, Dixon Hall, with the help of volunteers from its community, has continued to create programmes with common goals: to strengthen the self-reliance of the individual, re-affirm the traditional virtues of the family, and give the community itself an increasing sense of identity and purpose.

PEOPLE AND PLACES

The following are the names of some of the many people who grew up in Cabbagetown or lived there for a substantial period of time, and who became prominent in their fields of endeavour:

Sports

Louis Carroll	football
Jack Sinclair	football
"Frenchy" Belanger	boxing—fly-weight, world champion
Larry Gaines	boxing—heavy-weight—Br. Empire champion
Charles Murphy	boxing—fly-weight, Canadian champion
George Young	long-distance swimmer

Three early pictures of Hugh Garner. Born in 1913, Hugh (known as 'Hubert' when these pictures were taken) was to chronicle his youth in Cabbagetown in his early novel, Cabbagetown, and in his autobiography One Damn Thing After Another. He left the district during the depression, and his subsequent career took him away from Cabbagetown, but his early experiences provided the well-spring of his writing. He never forgot his struggle to rise above the poverty of his youth. One of his Cabbagetown friends once remarked to him, "I don't see how in hell you ever became a novelist, Hubie. Nobody from our old neighbourhood ever became a novelist!"

—Jean McFarlane, Hugh's Sister.

Art and Literature

Fred Varley	artist
C.W. Jeffreys	artist and illustrator
Ernest Thompson Seton	writer
Sir Charles G.D. Roberts	writer
Hugh Garner	writer
Gordon Sinclair	writer, broadcaster
Owen Staples	artist
Walter Allward	sculptor
George Brigden	artist
Sir Ernest MacMillan	musician
Walter Huston	movie producer, director, author

Business

William Gooderham	distiller
James Worts	miller
James Gooderham Worts	distiller
Sir Henry Pellatt	financier
John Taylor	J. & J. Taylor Safes
Peter Freyseng	Freyseng Cork Co.
Oronhyatekha	head of Independent Order of Foresters
John Ross Robertson	editor, philanthropist
Alfred Mills	Chairman Mills
James Grand	Grand & Toy
Samuel Toy	Grand & Toy
H.W. Bacon	H.W. Bacon Cartage
Bill, Ed. and Alex Robertson	Robertson Bros. Chocolates
G.W. Wood	Wood Gundy
James Ryrie	Ryrie—Birks
Milton Cork	president of Loblaws Groceterias
Enoch Turner	brewer
Larry McGuiness	McGuiness Distillery
Herb and Barry Milne	Milne's Fuels

Other

Charles Unwin	City Surveyor
Roland Michener	Gov. Gen. of Canada
Joseph Sedgwick	lawyer

Mayors

Robert J. Fleming	(1892-93, 1896-97)
Emerson Coatsworth	(1906-07)
Joseph Oliver	(1908-09)
Horatio C. Hocken	(1912-14)
Thomas Church	(1915-21)
Thomas Foster	(1925-27)

BUSINESSES

The following are brief historical descriptions of a few of the businesses which began in or had early connections with Cabbagetown:

Carhartt Ltd

Manufacturers of workwear and denim clothing, Carhartt's began operation in about 1888 at 535 Queen Street East, two doors west of King. At one time the factory employed one hundred people. Surviving a bankruptcy, in 1939, the company was revived by a Mr. Morawetz. Later, in 1960, it moved to a new location on River Street, just north of Queen, and operated there until 1981, when the company moved to Unionville.

Dalton's (1834) Limited

In 1834, Henry Dalton established a soap factory and candle business in London, Ontario. In 1849, his sons, James, Charles, and Joshua, took over the business, calling it Dalton Brothers. In 1873, the firm moved to Toronto, its first location here being at 151 Front Street East, where it also sold coffee. In 1892, it expanded the coffee part of the business, adding such commodities as potash, and ceased making candles. It operated this way in various sites until 1936, when it began to sell such things as spices, extracts, mustard, jelly and lemonade powders. In 1936 it moved to 226 Front Street, and started a processing factory for maraschino cherries. In 1938, it was taken over by a company owned by H.W. Grierson, which had formerly sold imported dates, the first to do so in Ontario. Under the name Dalton's (1834) Limited, adopted in 1940, the firm moved to its recent location at an old gas works building, 237-43 Front Street East, in 1967.

Davies Meat Packing

In 1861, William Davies established in Toronto the first factory in Canada devoted to the curing and smoking of meat, at the south west corner of Front and Frederick (later part of the Taylor Safe building). His business prospered, and in 1874 he built a large plant on Front Street East near the Don River. By 1877 the company was shipping 250,000 hogs annually, and had begun to open retail stores for the sale of meat products, having eighty-four of them across Ontario by the 1880's. By the 1890s Davies was supplying one-half of the entire Canadian bacon trade with England, and had become the largest pork-packing company in the British Empire. The large number of pigs being herded to the stock yards for the Davies' company, led to the name "Hogtown" being applied generally to Toronto. In 1927 a new company was formed to acquire and consolidate a number of meat-packing concerns, foremost of which was Davies'. This company was called Canada Packers. To-day many of the old Davies', buildings still stand. Flying over them to this day is the flag of Canada Packers.

Gendron Industries Ltd

Established in 1875, Gendron was a manufacturer of high quality bicycles, baby carriages, strollers and similar items. In the 1890s, it moved from Wellington Street to a new factory at the south west corner of Richmond and Ontario Streets. At that time it was one of the largest manufacturing concerns in Canada, and continued to produce its wares until 1982, when high interest rates and a depressed economy drove it to close down its Cabbagetown operations.

Gerhard Heintzman Limited

A number of members of the Heintzman family of Toronto were involved in the manufacture of pianos, several in the west-end Junction district. In the 1860s, Gerhard Heintzman founded a factory for this purpose, which in 1892 moved to a large building on the east side of Sherbourne Street, north of Adelaide, previously used by the Toronto Electric Light Company. By 1903, the business had proven so successful that it built a second factory south of the first, extending the Heintzman complex all the way down to Adelaide. The factory, employing 250 workmen, made a large selection of excellent pianos, which proved popular throughout the world. To-day, the factory still stands on Sherbourne. Although painted over in red, it still displays the original wall-lettering on the brick courses between the window rows, by which the company first advertised its name and products.

Meech's Meat Market

In the 1880s, Charlie Meech came from England to Toronto, and found employment at Stone's butcher shop, on Parliament at Carlton, now the site of Home Hardware. In time, he took over the store, and by World War II Meech's Meat Market had become one of the largest butcher shops in Toronto, serving, among other areas, Rosedale. His son, Richard Meech, although trained as a butcher, later went on to university.

Behind the store was a stable for ten horses and a similar number of delivery wagons, displaying the slogan "Obtain good health through good living. Buy your meat at Charlie Meech's." In the fall, hunters would bring in their deer, bear and other birds and animals for preparation by Charlie Meech. At this time of the year, in common with other butcher stores, Meech's would have such animals hanging out on meathooks for display to the buying public. As with other family business establishments, the family lived over the store.

Chairman Mills

Until 1907, W.S. Mills worked for a fashionable furniture store which also from time to time loaned out chairs to its customers for use on special occasions such as parties. From this he developed the idea of setting up a business to rent out chairs, and after his employer's business had been sold, he purchased its horse and wagon, and the chairs which had previously been used for loan. He made up business cards, reading: "W.S. Mills—Chairs for Hire", and charged three cents per chair, including delivery and pick-up. The name "Chairman Mills" was coined by his friend A.W. Miles, a funeral home proprietor, who would steer business to him when extra chairs were needed for funerals.

W.S. Mills died in 1936, and his son Alfred later took over the successful business and, except for a brief period of "retirement", has been in charge ever since.

Nettleship's Hardware

The building at 576 Parliament Street was built in 1876 as a rooming house. In 1920-21, J.H. Nettleship founded a plumbing store there, under the name J.H. Nettleship and Son. The family resided in rooms over the store. The company soon expanded into hardware, and has been operating as a family business throughout the subsequent years of Cabbagetown's history.

Tidy's Flowers

Stephen Tidy came from Rochester, England, and in 1874, opened a small commercial greenhouse at 475 Ontario Street, which remained in operation until 1892-93. In 1877, a retail store was added at the front of the greenhouse. Later a larger greenhouse was acquired, at premises later known as 490 Ontario Street, just north of Carlton. To-day, Tidy's is one of Toronto's best known florists.

Rosar-Morrison Funeral Home

Founded in 1861 by a Mr. Solleder, the company's first funeral home was on King Street, between Power Street and the Don River. Frans Rosar married Mr. Solleder's daughter, and eventually took over the business. In the early 1900s they moved to the north west corner of Sherbourne and Shuter Streets. More recently the funeral home was moved to its present location at 467 Sherbourne Street, where it carries on business in an old house built by Senator Stanley Cox as a present for his daughter. Tom Morrison married John (Bud) Rosar's daughter in 1955, and became associated with the business at that time, later purchasing the company after the death of Bud Rosar, and adding his own name to the title. John Morrison, the present proprietor represents the sixth generation in what has been called "Toronto's oldest family-owned funeral home".

Walkin Shoes

It seems an amazing coincidence that a shoe store should be operated by a family named Walkin, thereby selling "Walkin Shoes", but that is the case with this family business concern, which was established in 1918 by Morris Walkin, in a store at the south east corner of Queen and Parliament. Moving to 267 Queen in 1920, 292 Queen in 1930 and 220 Queen in 1948, (when it also had three branches in outlying areas), the shoe store, operated since 1945 by Irv Walkin, son of the founder, came to its present store, 246 Parliament Street, in 1968, where it sells inexpensive shoes by retail and wholesale.

Charles Wilson Ltd

Established in Toronto in 1875, this well-known Canadian manufacturer of non-intoxicating beverages has acquired an international reputation for its ginger ales and other soft drinks. Coming to Toronto from Montreal, its first factory here was a 2 storey roughcast building between Bleecker and Sherbourne Streets, north of Wellesley. By 1893, Wilson's had four bottling machines in operation in a larger factory on the same site, employing twenty-two people, and producing annually seventy-five to one hundred thousand dozen bottles of "temperance" beverages, and winning many awards for the excellent quality of its product. Very early in its history, it adopted a trade mark which has become well-known to millions—a squirrel holding a nut.

Morris Walkin, founder of Walkin Shoes, in 1918, stands in front of his store at 267 Queen Street West, in 1920.

—*Irv Walkin, Walkin Shoes*

Fire truck leaving No. 4 station, Berkeley and Adelaide Streets, 1923.

—*Toronto, Reflections of the Past, Mike Filey, 1972.*

PLACES

There are many buildings and places of interest throughout the area south of Bloor between Sherbourne and the Don. A map in this book shows the location of many of them, including all of those listed on the inventory of the Toronto Historical Board. The following are brief descriptions of a few of the more interesting ones:

2 Berkeley Street
Built in various stages between 1868 and 1910, this was the Toronto Knitting and Yarn Factory, established by Joseph Simpson, in 1868. The building, designed by C.J. Gibson, recently underwent extensive renovations by architect Jack Diamond, as part of a new "Berkeley Castle" retail and commercial complex.

37 Metcalfe Street, 1892, seen from the north west.

—The Canadian Architect and Builder, 1892.

37 Metcalfe Street, as it looked in 1982, showing the west facade. The original entrance to the first part of the house still faces north, *into the south wall of the Hampton Mansions apartment buildings.*
—*George H. Rust-D'Eye*

192 Carlton Street. One of the oldest buildings in this part of the city, this house was built for A. McLean Howard, in 1850, when Carlton, then spelt with an "E", was a tree-lined country road. The photo was taken early in this century. —Second Mile Club

70 Berkeley Street

Several firehalls in Toronto have been recycled for other purposes. Lombard Street Station became a dinner theatre, Bellevue a museum, and an 1870's hose tower projects from the top of the St. Charles Tavern on Yonge Street. No. 4 Firehall, on Berkeley Street at its south west corner of Adelaide, is now a theatre. The original firehall on the site was built in 1859, and rebuilt, under A.F. Wickson, architect, in 1885-86; this structure, in turn, was replaced by the present 1905 building. In 1970-71, the firehall was saved from demolition, by the University Alumnae Dramatic Club, and is now a 154-seat theatre, designed by architect Ron Thom.

95 Berkeley Street

This handsome 1906 building once housed the stables of the Christie Biscuit Factory, which in 1874 moved downtown from Yorkville to a site on the south side of Adelaide Street east of George. For many years it was the truck depot and stables for the horses used to pull the Christie's delivery wagons. Near the top of the building on the south side is a beam and pulley that was used to hoist the heavy bales of hay for the horses. A few years ago, the old stable was acquired and renovated by Adcom Research Inc.

192 Carlton Street

One of the oldest houses in the area, this large brick dwelling was constructed in 1850 for A. McLean Howard, clerk of the First Division Court, and well-known benefactor to many of the Anglican churches in the area, including All Saints', St. Bartholomew's, and nearby St. Peter's, which stands on land which he once owned. When the house was built, there were forests in the area north of Carlton to Howard Street, and a natural swimming hole in a stream at Allan Gardens. Carlton was a pleasant tree-lined country road, along which Mr. Howard rode his horse to work. Thirty-six years later, horse-cars were introduced on Carlton.

In 1947 the house, which had been modified in 1910, was acquired by the city and leased to the Second Mile Club.

295 Carlton Street

This handsome yellow-brick Victorian Gothic house was built in 1878-79 for Hugh Neilson, first Toronto manager of the Dominion Telegraph Company, and later, in 1879, superintendent of the Telephone Despatch Company, which was later acquired by the Bell Telephone Company. One of the first telephones in Toronto was installed in this house.

308 and 314 Carlton Street
the "Brick houses"

A prominent house-builder in the Don Vale and other areas of the City, and chief contractor for the gas works site on Eastern Avenue, Benjamin Brick built and lived in, first 314 Carlton (1875), and then 308 Carlton (1890). Both show the craftsmanship and individualism which characterized his work. On No. 314, a second Empire-style cottage, the dormer windows in the fish-scaled mansard roof are set over the spaces between the first floor bays, achieving a degree of harmony not found on many buildings of that size. When Benjamin Brick built 308 Carlton, he had just returned from a visit to Paris, France, where he was inspired by the workmanship and artistic forms in some of the houses he had seen. This led him to create richly decorated plaster mouldings and an exquisite dining room ceiling. That dining room, at the south west corner of the house, is one of the most ornate and interesting rooms in this part of the city. A similar ceiling was executed at 282 Carlton Street. Benjamin Brick also built in the area, no.'s 255, 257 and 259 Carlton Street. In the period 1923-25, 308 Carlton housed a branch of the Toronto Conservatory of Music.

Benjamin Brick, his wife, and their daughter, Elizabeth, c. 1870. Elizabeth did not live long after the taking of this picture but the couple had five more children, all of whom lived well into this century. Benjamin Brick was a builder and contractor who left 308 and 314 Carlton, and 15 other houses in his estate when he died in 1913.
— *Chubb Family Collection*

Don Station

A small picturesque railway station was built in 1889 at the C.P.R. level crossing at Queen Street on the west side of the Don. In 1911, when Queen Street was elevated to go over the Don River, the station remained where it was, but in the shadow of the bridge.

In 1915, several hundred young men and their sweethearts crowded the station and its platform, saying good-bye, as the boys went off to war. These were the soldiers of the fifteenth battalion of the 48th Highlanders Regiment, on their way to the second battle of Ypres, where poison gas was first used, by the German army. In this battle, every member of the battalion was killed, wounded or taken prisoner.

In 1969, the station was moved to its present site at Todmorden Mills.

37 Metcalfe Street and Hampton Mansions

In 1875, a two-storey farmhouse-type of dwelling was built by John Douglas, on the south side of Winchester Street, just east of Metcalfe. Numbered 75 Winchester, and set well back from the street on its spacious lot, this attractive house had a beautiful front doorway, with large wooden doors glazed with cut and etched glass. By 1883, the house was owned by James L. Morrison, who, in 1891, carried out the first major renovations, including the addition to its exterior of large verandahs and carved wooden railings, and a high widow's walk on top of the roof. This modernization, executed by architect J. Wilson Gray, made the old house almost unrecognizable.

By 1912, Alexander Park had acquired the house and was building to the north of it the first of two large yellow brick apartment buildings, later to be known as Hampton Mansions. In 1912, the old house, now hidden from view to Winchester Street, underwent its second set of major changes, which oriented its principal facade to Metcalfe Street, moved around many of the architectural features from the 1891 work, and erected a west wall bearing such a mish-mash of architectural forms as to astonish and baffle architects and neighbours alike. Now known as 37 Metcalfe Street, it is one of the most unusual houses in the City. It has recently undergone yet another set of radical renovations and restoration work, including the acquisition of the beautiful old metal fence which previously graced the now-demolished Ports of Call, on Yonge Street.

417-425 Parliament Street

This was the factory of the J.G. Gibson Marble Works, established in 1868, the first steam works in the City.

494 Ontario Street

Built in 1905, this small building was the first church of the Christian Association. Later known as the Backdoor Theatre, it was left unused during the destruction of surrounding buildings for the south of St. Jamestown housing development. It still stands vacant, awaiting a new use, probably as a senior citizens' centre.

547 Parliament Street·

Built in 1906, this building first housed part of the Gibson Marble Works and later a maker of medical glass, known as Beaver Flint Glass. In 1945 it became a ladies' foundation garment factory, and later, as Essentials Manufacturing Limited, also made babies' clothes. In 1975 it was renovated as a restaurant, named Bobbins, a reference to the needlework which had once been done there.

19 River Street

Erected in 1905, it was the home of one of several vinegar producers in the area, Queen City Vinegar Company.

56 Rose Avenue

A house which faced south when it was built in the 1850s, it is now the side entrance to the east which faces out to the street. In 1878 it received extensive modifications by builder George Hardy, including the addition of a high Victorian decorated tower to what had previously been a late Georgian-style dwelling.

377 Sackville Street

A large imposing Second Empire house, built in 1876-77, its attractive presence on the street is magnified by the gray stone facing, which would make it look at home in a provincial town in France. Otherwise, it is essentially similar to its neighbours to the south, also erected by Bruce and Hagon, builders.

291 Sherbourne Street

This large Victorian dwelling was, from 1881 until his death in 1918, the home of John Ross Robertson, writer, historian, editor and philanthropist. Founder of the *Evening Telegram* in 1876, and principal contributor to the founding of Sick Children's Hospital, (1892), he is perhaps best known for his six-volume set of books, *Robertson's Landmarks of Toronto* based on articles written in his newspaper, which he published from 1894 to 1914, and for the gigantic collection of historical material which he left to the Toronto Public Library.

35 Spruce Street

An early 1860's house, this small brick late-Georgian cottage was first lived in by a postmaster. Although a farmhouse-style dwelling, it was never a farmhouse.

56 Spruce Street

This early 1870s home was until recently one of the least changed from its original appearance of all of the houses in this part of the city. It is still a fine example of an early frame rough-cast working class dwelling.

384 Sumach Street

Known locally as 'the Witch's house', this attractive small building, erected c.1866, probably comes closest to matching everyone's impression of how a Victorian house should look. Of pleasing proportions, it was carefully constructed, with much more detail and attention to decorative craftmanship than characterized most buildings of this size.

314 Wellesley Street East

Built in 1890 and suitably sighted on high ground, this delightful house is a catalogue of the Victorian decorative forms that typify the Don Vale area. Among the more whimsical of the decorations is a small serpent in the highest gable and a stylized sun over the door. There is also an extensive use of terra cotta tiles. The house has recently been restored, and is obviously well cared for.

402½ Wellesley Street East

Known throughout the area as the Owl House because of the small masonry owl on the wall under one of its windows, this peculiar and whimsical little house was built in 1892-93 by Charles T. Jeffreys, for his son Charles W. Jeffreys, the outstanding commercial artist, historian and illustrator whose publications included the *Picture Gallery of Canadian History,* and who, like his fellow artist, Owen Staples, drew many of the sketches for *Robertson's Landmarks.* Apparently the house once had a third floor. It is one of the delightful "hidden houses" of the area, although not as hidden as it was before it donated the name for the development around it, Owl House Lane.

Wellesley Cottages

If there is an indigenous form of Ontario architecture, it must be the labourers' cottage, the 1½ storey, centre hall plan small house, with

56 Rose Avenue, in about 1880. This is the south facade of an 1850's house to which a late 1870's tower had just been added. Its original address was on Prospect Street, not Rose, to which its side now faces.
— *City of Toronto Archives Ref. 9.2.3G 799*

The buildings of the P.R. Lamb Glue and Blacking Manufactory, at the end of Amelia Street, East of Sumach, looking south, c. 1880. In the centre background can be seen the spire of the Necropolis Chapel.

—City of Toronto Archives, Lamb Collection 76 9.2.3G 794 Reprinted with the permission of Dorothy Lamb.

The remains of the P.R. Lamb Manufactory after the fire on May 20th, 1888 which put an end to its business. The firm had many life-long employees, some of whom lived in small houses in the area. Some of these were owned by Lamb's and rented to workers. The factory buildings were grossly underinsured, so the fire was devastating to employer and employee alike.

—City of Toronto Archives: Lamb Collection Print]78

one window on each side of the door and often a central gable projecting from the attic storey. This design won an architectural award in a competition for a design for a workman's cottage at the Crystal Palace Exhibition in London in 1851,[29] and from that time until the 1890s, thousands of them in various sizes and degrees of amenity, were constructed throughout the downtown area of Toronto.

Wellesley Cottages, which is the name of the street, as well as the houses which are on it, is an interesting small development of labourers' cottages, "off the beaten track", north of Wellesley Street East, west of Sackville. There are seven of them, built in 1886-87, on a little laneway which, with its trees, adds an air of rural charm to this little enclave of tranquility in the middle of a populous neighbourhood.

Until recently, the cottages were in common ownership, as was the street, which in winter might be flooded for a skating rink. Gloria Rankin, who lived in one of the cottages as a young girl, remembers that once in a while a child digging at the far end of the yard would come across bones washed down from the cemetery behind the cottages.

71 Winchester Street

One of a number of houses built on the south side of Winchester west of Metcalfe in about 1890 this house was, from 1920 to the late 1930s, operated as a private hospital, known as the Coronado. The proprietress was Mrs. Falby, assisted by Mrs. Lloyd.

A wedding gathering at 156 Winchester Street in the early 1900s.

In the centre, front row are Daniel Lamb, (with child on knee), Annie Millen, and Eliza Lamb. —Dorothy Lamb, Family Collection.

156 Winchester Street

Parts of this beautiful house contain the oldest architectural elements in the area, dating to the 1830s. This was the house of Daniel Lamb, who on the day of his wedding to Eliza Lumbers, on May 1, 1867, moved with his bride into the newly expanded and renovated house.

Daniel Lamb was the son of Peter Rothwell Lamb, who came to Toronto in 1834. In 1848, he established the P.R. Lamb Manufactory in what is now Hillcrest Park, at the end of Amelia Street, then in the suburbs. This factory, which produced various well-known products such as Lamb's Penny (Stove) Blacking, and Lamb's Glue, expanded quickly. It consisted of about a dozen buildings when, on May 20, 1888 it burned to the gound. This fire, the second suffered by the factory, put an end to its business there, because while Lamb's had given employment to the area and contributed to its development, nevertheless by 1888 the area was too built-up to tolerate a glue factory at the end of the street.

Peter Lamb was also, with Joseph Workmen, one of the founders of the Unitarian Church of Canada.

His son, Daniel, born in 1842, took over the glue and blacking business from his father in the 1860s. However, he was also interested in politics, serving as alderman for St. David's Ward in 1885-86, for Ward 2 in 1895-1902, and on the Board of Control, in 1897, 1898 and 1901. He has been credited with responsibility for many improvements in the city, including the Riverdale Zoo, Rosedale Valley Road, the water works at the Island, the reclaiming of Ashbridge's Bay, and the provision of main railway throughfares from the east end.

Daniel and Eliza Lamb's house still stands today, at 156 Winchester Street. It is set well back from the street, although its grounds are not quite as spacious as they once were, after the building of houses at the corners of the property in 1903. What can be seen to-day are parts of an 1830s house, as expanded and renovated in 1867 and 1877. Most of the front facade is from the latter date. There once was a carriage stepping-stone out at the curb, and a beautiful Victorian picket fence, designed by architect Henry Langley. Within the last few years a new fence has been erected, including an attractive wooden gate, each a perfect replica of the original.

Winchester Street House—This was one of two similar houses which stood on the north side of Winchester Street between Metcalfe and Sackville Streets, from 1855 to the late 1880's. This was the home of Edward Cooper, dry goods dealer. It was located a short distance east of Metcalfe. The design of the fence and gate is attributed to architect Henry Langley.

—Russell Cooper

CABBAGETOWN'S OLDEST BUILDINGS

On the basis of available records, the following, in order, are the oldest buildings in the area under discussion:

Little Trinity Church, S.W. King and Trinity: 1843
Derby Tavern, S.E. Parliament and King: 1846-7
houses built by Paul Bishop, 363-65 Adelaide St. E.: 1848
A. McLean Howard house, 192 Carlton Street: 1850
36 Metcalfe Street, built for William Hannah: 1852
Little Trinity Rectory, 417 King St. East: 1853
399-403 King Street East: 1855
435 Sackville Street, (rear), built for John Eastwood: 1856
331-43 Seaton Street (houses): 1857
85 Winchester Street, first resident, Samuel Lyn: 1857
Chapel of St. James-the-Less, Parliament Street: 1858
The Don Jail, Gerrard Street East, east of the Don: designed 1858
"Allendale", 241 Sherbourne Street, house of Enoch Turner: c. 1858
285-7 Sherbourne Street, 1858
Francy Barn — Riverdale Farm: 1858 (moved here from Markham)
261 Sherbourne Street, James Small house: c. 1859
56 Rose Avenue, (house): c. 1858, 1878
77 Seaton Street, (house): late 1850s
Palace Street School, S.E. Front and Cherry Streets, 1859
302 King Street East, (originally a tavern): c. 1860
136-40 Seaton Street, (houses): 1860
35 Spruce Street c. 1861
185 Carlton Street, (house): c. 1860-65
21 Winchester Street, house of Rev. Samuel Boddy: c. 1863
230-32 Carlton Street, (houses): 1864
St. Peter's Church, Carlton Street: 1865
Lamb House — Winchester Street: 1867, 1877

The Scadding cabin, at the Canadian National Exhibition Grounds, started off life in 1796 on the east side of the Don, near Queen, from where it was moved to the Exhibition Grounds in 1879.

PLAQUES ON HISTORIC BUILDINGS

Province of Ontario

Enoch Turner Schoolhouse
Little Trinity Church
Allan Gardens
John Ross Robertson (at 291 Sherbourne St.)

Toronto Historical Board

Prince Edward Viaduct
Toronto General Hospital
(Spruce Street, east of Sackville)
Simpson Farmhouse (Riverdale Farm)
Winchester School
St. Peter's Church
Trinity College Medical School
Sackville Street Public School

Don Valley Conservation Authority

Castle Frank

Government of Canada

George Brown Tomb, Necropolis Cemetery

STREET NAMES

A number of streets in Cabbagetown and its surrounding area have had their names changed from time to time. Some of these changes caused confusion. For instance, King Street was first applied to the southernmost street in the Town, then transferred one street north to what was then Duke Street which in turn moved one north to supplant Newgate. Parliament Street was first applied to what is now Berkeley Street.

Queen Street was Lot Street; Trinity was Windmill; Eastern was Park; parts of Ontario were McMahon; Gerrard was Don and Danforth Road; Richmond was first Hospital, then Duchess; Rose was North Berkeley; Dundas, at various times and sections was Wilton, Beech or Cruikshank; Prospect was Nassau; Sackville was Pine; Carlton was Elm; Aberdeen was at different times Carlton or Lamb; Shuter was Sydenham or North Park; Sherbourne was Caroline. Many of these changes occurred relatively recently.

Both Carlton and Sherbourne are misspelled; according to their derivations they should be Carleton and Sherborne respectively Princess should be Princes.

From time to time street numberings also were changed, with most of the last ones occurring in the late 1880s. As mementoes of the previous numbering, the stained glass in the transoms of 177 and 179 Seaton show their original numbers, 125 and 127 respectively. Similarly, 413 and 417 Sackville show 341 and 345 in their transom glass.

383 Shuter Street, 1937, then known as 99½ Sydenham Street. Then and until its upper floors were added in 1981 it was the smallest house in the city. Built 1885-90, at 8' 3'' it is still the narrowest.
—*City of Toronto Archives Ref. D.P.W.]33-143*

With the destruction of approximately eight hundred houses for Regent Park, and because of other projects which had led to the large-scale demolition of houses, Cabbagetown has lost almost all of the little cul-de-sacs which once were so much a part of its character. A few, such as Gilead Place, and, appropriately, Virgin Street, still exist as names but no longer have any houses on them. However, many of them have simply disappeared.

The following is a list of some of the small Cabbagetown streets which have vanished without a trace: Central Row, Coatsworth Lane, Armstrong Avenue, William Street, Roslin Avenue, Lima Street, Otter Avenue, Reed Street, Home Place, Ontario Place, Maple Row, Oland Place, Wilmot Avenue, Clara Street, Orford Avenue, Dean Street, Hanover Place, and Melady's Lane.

Darling Terrace, 1877, 562-6 Parliament Street, detail and plaque
—George Rust-D'Eye

Detail, 224 Queen Street East
—George H. Rust-D'Eye

DID YOU KNOW?

Miscellaneous facts about Cabbagetown:

—You can often tell a Cabbagetowner by the way he or she pronounces the name of Sumach Street; old-timers pronounce it: shoo-mack.

—the narrowest house in the city, formerly the smallest before the addition of upper floors, is 383 Shuter Street, built c. 1885-90. It measures eight feet, three inches across.

—The house at 5 Rose Avenue, part of an 1879 terrace of small brick dwellings, is actually a replica of a previous house which was extracted from the row during the "blockbusting" for south of St. Jamestown. Another house, not such an exact replica, but with a somewhat similar background, is to be found at 92 Ontario Street.

—several significant changes in Cabbagetown seem to have been brought about by the Victorian equivalent of ratepayer protests: the building of Little Trinity Church and Enoch Turner Schoolhouse, and the preservation for public use of Moss Park and part of Riverdale Park south of the Necropolis.

—in 1911, a Civic Improvement Committee made a number of recommendations to City Council, among which was the laying out of a diagonal street, or "radial thoroughfare" from the intersection of Queen and Church streets to the corner of Carlton and Parliament. Fortunately for a lot of homeowners in the path of that swath, the recommendation was never adopted.

—the houses at 306B and 308B Wellesley Street East are joined at the second floor level over a common carriageway.

—the handsome building with the turret at the north east corner of Parliament and Amelia, built in 1889 for Barr's Dairy, still has the name of that company in elegant letters imbedded in its doorstep.

—dotted throughout the Cabbagetown area, and in other parts of the city, are a number of carefully-detailed cast iron manhole covers dated 1889. Locations of two of them are north east corner of Metcalfe and Carlton; south east corner of Sackville and Winchester.

Public lavatories at the south-west corner of Queen and Parliament Streets, 1913. These facilities, are similar to ones at Broadview and Queen, recently removed and lodged with the Toronto Historical Board. The ones shown quickly became the subject matter of a lawsuit, with the Supreme Court of Canada awarding damages against the city for injurious affection. The johns constituted a nuisance!

To the north in the picture is the newly-named and quite respectable Rupert Hotel.

—City of Toronto Archives D.P.W. 55-36

—the strangely-angled brick buildings at 362-64 King Street East, built by Robert Paul, a cab owner and grocer, in 1874, have a plaque attesting to the fact on the front. On the rear of one of them is a strange, clean chevron-shaped patch on the otherwise dirty brick. This marks the former location of a very old enclosed wooden stairway, which was removed a few years ago.

—there are a number of other buildings in the Cabbagetown area bearing dated plaques, some with the name of the building or its builder. Some of these are : 165-79 Carlton Street: "Chamberlin Block, 1877"; 443-43 Parliament Street: "Lepper's Block 1885"; 562-66 Parliament Street: "Darling Terrace, 1877"; 376 Sackville Street: "Pine Terrace 1886"; and "Sackville Street Public School, 1887". At the north east corner of Metcalfe and Winchester streets, sitting on the ground, is a peculiar stone from an old building, dated on three sides: 1881, 1903 and 1906.

—the commercial row building at 224 Queen Street has the likeness of a sheep carved in masonry on the second floor.

—many of the old houses built in Cabbagetown in the 1870s and 1880s had elaborate wrought iron cresting (small ornamental fences), along their roofs and first-storey bays. Many also originally had ornamental iron fences around their properties. Much of this Victoriana was lost to the scrap drives during the two World Wars. A good example of cresting is still to be found on the northernmost of the magnificent row of Second Empire houses, built by John Bowden, on the west side of Parliament just below Winchester, (1876).

—building permits were not required until 1887 and even then many small developments were built without them. There were not at that time any zoning by-laws or set-back requirements. As a result some houses built in the middle of their estates later sold off land around them to developers, and because many houses had large stables or coach houses out behind, a number of old houses now stand in the middle of blocks, or behind other houses. Examples may be seen at 21 Winchester, 254 Carlton, 44 Amelia, 395 and 435 Sackville, and houses behind 524-34 Queen Street, 48-50 Spruce Street and 141 Berkeley Street.

—as previously mentioned, the Cabbagetown area was originally in St. David's Ward and St. Lawrence's Ward, in 1834. After the Liberties were absorbed, in 1859, St. Thomas's Ward was split off from St. David's west of Ontario Street. In 1891, numbered "strip" wards came in, and the whole area was included in Ward 2 west of Sumach, and Ward 1 east of Sumach. In 1969 it all became part of Ward 7.

—Albert Franck (1899-1973) the well-known painter of street scenes and back lanes of Toronto did much of his work in the Cabbagetown area, including some of his best-known works *The Black House* (441 Ontario Street), and *Backyard on Carlton* (the rear of 295 Carlton, with 280 Carlton across the street).

—in 1912, the City of Toronto built underground public lavatories in the sidewalk at the south west corner of Parliament and Queen. The owners of the store at that location, J.F. Brown Company, sued the City, alleging that the installation of the facilities had caused depreciation to its property value. The case went to the Supreme Court of Canada,[30] resulting in a judgment against the City in the amount of nine thousand dollars. This probably explains why the City of Toronto, unlike civilized cities throughout the world, has so few public conveniences.

Epilogue

Where is Cabbagetown?

Before any answer can be given to that question, it is necessary to decide: does Cabbagetown exist to-day at all?

While it may not be totally acceptable to adopt the feeling of some of the old-timers that Cabbagetown died after World War I, there is no doubt that the war shattered many of the foundations of its previous vitality. Much of the strength of Cabbagetown depended on its youth; the War took the young people away, many of them never to return. Much of the stability of Cabbagetown depended on the reassurance provided by the family; the War broke up families. And much of the durability of Cabbagetown depended on common ties of kinship, socio-economic class, nationality, religion, and philosophy; the War brought change in the composition of the neighbourhoods; many absentee landlords took in disreputable single roomers, and allowed their houses to become run down; and the new industrialization and mobility accompanying the War years irretrievably altered the fabric of life in what had formerly been a vibrant, though poor, community.

There is a marked difference in the approaches to Cabbagetown by Bill Hambly and J.V. McAree, who lived there before the War, and Hugh Garner, who came there afterward. The latter seems to have wanted to use the word "slum" in conjunction with Cabbagetown at every available opportunity. Many of the old-timers from the pre-War period, (what has been called "the golden years"), as well as many of those who lived there since, take serious issue with his insistence on the application of this term to their community. Many point out that he lived there for only three years, and never tried to find out what the area was all about. While acknowledging the obvious fact that everyone in Cabbagetown was poor, they point out that Cabbagetowners had pride in their city, their country, and themselves, and that their own self-respect would not tolerate their environment becoming a slum. It was a working class community, of honest, simple people, who worked hard and tried to keep their houses clean; it was not a slum.

Perhaps it was this pride which was injured by the War. And if the spirit and tradition of Cabbagetown survived the Great War, it was struck a resounding blow by the Depression. Vitality was sapped, optimism drained. No one had a job. No one had anything. Having survived relative poverty for so long, the prospect of no possibility for improvement added greatly to the divisive factors which had come with the War and were still having their effects.

However, the fact that so many people still feel pride in having lived in Cabbagetown, and that so many later Torontonians, touched by this feeling, want to become part of Cabbagetown tradition, are conclusive signs that Cabbagetown did not die after the First World War nor immediately after the Second. But what the War did to the spirit of the original Cabbagetown, the Regent Park Housing development and other initiatives of "urban renewal", did to its physical fabric.

Although many of those who lived in the area before 1949, moved into new accommodation there afterward, nevertheless the unique blend of factors that made up Cabbagetown could never again be recreated: the North of Ireland way of life, the small, old houses, the dead-end streets, the strong sense of "we" and "they", the tolerance to deplorable health and housing conditions, the feeling of caring for one's family and others in the neighbourhood, the joy of sharing simple pleasures with friends and neighbours, the corner stores, the horses, the streetcars, the sounds, the smells, the poverty, the Orange Lodge, the central role of the church—all of these, as well as the geographical location of Cabbagetown and its history, contributed in some important way to the tradition which was Cabbagetown. Wherever these factors existed, Cabbagetown existed.

Cabbagetown lives in the hearts of those who dwelt there and in the minds of those who understand the reasons for their pride.

Where is Cabbagetown? It doesn't matter, for all of it is history.

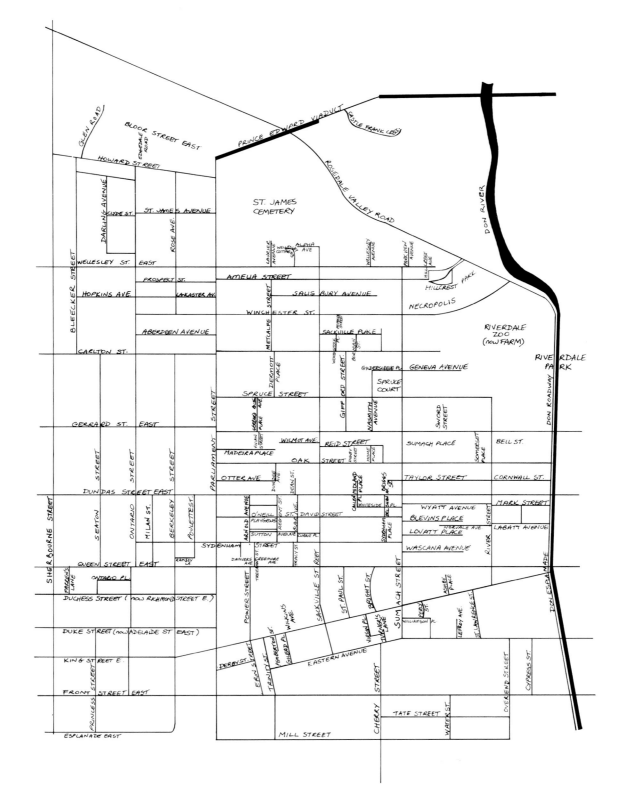

A Walking Tour
Through Old Cabbagetown

Cabbagetown observer and raconteur, James J. Ealey has prepared the following description of what one would see on a walk through Cabbagetown in the 1930's. It is told in his own words:

"What was it really like?? Well, let's see . . .

As you leave the Old Shamrock Hotel at River and Gerrard you find yourself looking at the oldest operating factory in the district. It is listed as Kemp's Manufacturing, later on to be known as General Steel Wares.

If it happens to be the summer season, when you arrive at River and Dundas you would in all probability gaze at the high tent that those evangelist followers have erected on the lot at the northeast corner. They would be there every summer for about 3 or 4 weeks.

Cutting across Dundas you would cast your eyes, as you headed east, on G.H. Woods, 'sanitation for the nation' plant; next to that we find Johnston's leather and tannery works, and as you cut through that little lane and headed for Mark Street you would have to pass by the Sterling Laundry plant.

At the bottom of Mark Street stands one of the city's most renowned breweries—Reinhardt's, and just west of the brewery stands the old Dominion Silk Mills. Just around the corner on River Street you will find the famed Buckley Cartage family.

Heading down River Street we stop at Labatt and gaze towards the old Crouse & Hind's plant, and just opposite on Defries stands the original Beekist Honey outfit.

Mr. Newton had a chocolate plant on River Street and us kids were really concerned about his goods. When you finally arrive at River and Queen you would cut across over to King and head straight for those sand pits at the old Sam McCord sand and gravel yard. That was quite a play-spot on any given day, especially on those hot summer days and nights, you sure could smell them; I am of course referring to the old horse slaughter house known as— Harris's.

Cutting back to River and Queen you would stop at the old horse's watering trough, have a quick wash and a drink, step around the old Bank of Nova Scotia building and glimpse at the famed Carhartt's overall plant which was right next door to the bank.

Crossing over to the north side of Queen you would stop and take a look at some of those dolls working their butts off at the New Method Laundry that was right on the corner of River and Queen. It was always a treat to sit and watch those laundry wagons, drawn by those beautiful looking horses that the laundry owned, as they started out on their daily delivery trips.

Sitting back some 100 feet from the sidewalk, just to the north of the laundry, sits a very large house with a high play-yard. It is number 28 River. This home is probably the most fevered and memorable establishment in the district. The sign on the building tells you that is it the EAST END DAY NURSERY.

You had to enter this building to meet the most wonderful of matrons anywhere. Her name was Mrs. McKenzie, a truly remarkable woman.

As you head north on River you stop for a minute or two outside of number 64, for it was here that the Doughty family once lived during the time of the famous Ambrose Small disappearance case.

Just north of 64 we find the Stewart Hartshorn blind factory. We then cut along Norval and take a short-cut through the cat's hole. (It would be real interesting to know how many of those "Old Cabbagetowners" up Winchester way ever heard of this famed short-cut??). After you have cut through that passing you find that you have arrived at the old Booth, Coulter Copper & Brass factory.

Cutting across Sumach and heading west on Sydenham you find yourself looking up at the largest public school in the British Empire; it is kown as Park School #2. The first Park School was built in the year 1853 on St. David's Street. It was used to house some of the returning veterans after the first world war.

As we hit Sydenham & Sackville we stop and take a quick look at the Roher's bottle concern. The renowned Public Bath House up the street at St. David's, and directly opposite sits the old Sackville Street Mission. At number 225 Sackville you will find the birthplace of the world famous Frenchy Belanger. Frenchy won the World's Flyweight Boxing Championship. It would also be interesting to know just how many of those pseudo-Cabbagetowners who are promoting the selling of Old Cabbagetown could tell their prospective buyers where the home of Larry Gains was. I doubt it very much if they even knew who he was, let alone know where he used to live in the district. Larry Gains was one of Canada's truly great boxing champions, he was as a matter of fact, the British Empire Heavyweight Champion and if his skin had been white instead of black he would have become the World's best. Before we leave Sydenham, we stop for a moment or two to take a look at the smallest house in the Dominion at that time. It was just 8 feet wide.

As we stand at the corner of Sackville and Queen looking

south, we can see that small Catholic school on the east side— Sacred Heart. On the south side of Queen looking west stands the famed St. Paul's original school.

Strolling west along Queen we come to the Quacker Candy Company. Now it wasn't their product that made this concern such a well known concern throughout the land; it was their girls softball team, the famed QUACKER GIRLS. What a team that was, bloomers and all.

Passing Tracy we come to Johnny Chriss's headquarters, St. Paul's Parish Hall. It was here that the micky and protestant kids learned the art of self-defence from Johnny, along with the principle of good citizenship.

Right next door you would find old Tom changing the attraction notices at the Rialto theatre. It could have been Tom Mix and John Gilbert on the double billing at that time.

Further west we stop and take a good look at Trefann. This street was destined, some 40 years later, to become one of the city's most celebrated political squabbles. Before we hit Parliament we stop and gaze at a poster of Douglas Fairbanks Sr. This ad tells us that he will be the star attraction at the Idle Hour tonight. The Idle Hour. Now I would like to hear those super salesman from Winchester area explain how this movie house got up there in Old Cabbagetown.

Heading up Parliament we have to pass the old Indian Artifact store. The old chief would tell us stories about Sitting Bull and Custer. Just to the north stood the Ocean Blend Tea Company. Remember? And then we would come up to Cabbagetown's top movie house— The Bluebell

Crossing at Dundas, you stare at the infamous #4 police station, and right next door stands the #7 fire hall. It was here that the last of the horse-drawn fire engines were used in Toronto.

We pass by two of the city's oldest places of worship as we hit Oak Street, they are namely the Oak United, and St. Giles. I should also mention, that we had passed by Father Pashler's Anglican church earlier, St. Bartholomews. As we hit Gerrard and Parliament we come in contact with the old Gerrard Hotel and the beautiful(?) Eclipse theatre.

Heading back south on Parliament we arrive at the south/west corner of Dundas and Parliament and there we find the neighborhood's most famous retail store—Michaelson's. Just to the south of the store stands the home of the Salvation Army. There are just not enough words available to relate the goodness that they do, and have done for everyone throughout this district.

We cut back through a lane that brings us to the back door of Ma's Bakery at Berkeley Street. Just to the north of the bakery you will find a truly conservative type place of learning, aptly called— Lord Dufferin School.

Crossing Dundas and heading south on Berkeley we pass by the Acme Farmer's Dairy concern. Berkeley Street was a very picturesque street in those days, and it contained many fine stately homes, it was also the home of Cabbagetown's only synagogue.

We continue south until we arrive at one of the city's most noted landmarks—The Berkeley Street Fire Hall. It was erected in 1905. Today—, it is the home of the oldest theatre company in Toronto, but when we were kids around there it was the home of a truly magnificent group of men who manned that fire-hall. Christmas after Christmas those men gave all of those kids in the neighbourhhod one truly "A Night to Remember" time with their Christmas party.

As you leave the fire hall your eyes pick up a row of houses on the east side of Berkeley. Now these houses are not just any old ordinary houses, for they had been classed as workmen's cottages when they were built in 1872, and believe it or not, but they were built on the bank of what was known then as Taddle's Creek which once flowed into the Toronto Bay.

I should mention here that you have entered probably Toronto's most historical sections, and that all of the buildings mentioned are still standing to this day.

Returning to Queen and Berkeley for the moment, we drop in at the old Berkeley Street Methodist Church originally built in 1871. It was here that Marmaduke Pearson, the grandfather of our former Prime Minister—Mike Pearson—was the pastor.

Those of you out there whose parents had Christie's deliver their famed biscuits to their favourite grocer can look upon what was once the stable for his horses. It was at 95 Berkeley.

We are now back at King and Berkeley and standing in front of Greenshield's Grocery Store. And what a history this store has.

A century ago it catered to the carriage trade of Toronto, but when we were kids we would sit outside, (we were never allowed in the store), and watch those chauffeur-driven Buicks, Packards and the famous Pierce-Arrows drive up to the front door of Greenshield's.

Leaving that world of opulence, we travel one short block south to Front Street and the world of the "coke pickers", but before we cross over to their territory, we stop at the southeast corner of Front and Berkeley and let our imaginations take us back to the year of 1797 for it was on this very corner that Upper Canada had it's first Parliament Buildings erected, and believe it or not, in the war of 1812 the American forces burnt them to the ground.

You are now in the world of the Consumer's Gas Company. This company took in several blocks of the district, but the most active one was the east wall on Berkeley below Front, for it was here that the "coke pickers" put in a 52-week year. If you were part of those "pickers" then you will never forget it, and for those who were fortunate enough to escape it, then just forget it. Period.

Directly across from the coke picking action stood one magnificent building, so beautifully Romanesque styled that one of the city's demolition companies refused to raze it, instead, they bought it.

Just below this building at the foot of Berkeley you will find the original Simpson Knitting Mills.

Directly across from the main portion of the gas company stood a very large field, it was called Gas House Park. It was bordered by King-Parliament-Front and Berkeley streets. In the summer it was a hotbed of softball action, and in the long, cold winters there was a hockey cushion, a pleasure skating area and a small wooden sleigh-ride stand was built by the city.

Right across from the park, looking east, you could cast your eyes on two of the district's older establishments, one was for pleasure, (and brawls), and the other was for labouring in. The one for pleasure was the old Derby House, and the one for labouring in was Schraeder's Valve Company.

As you come to the corner of Power and King your eyes wander north until they focus on the old House of Providence complex and its vast grounds. This was the fore-runner of the beautiful Providence Villa up at Warden and St. Clair avenues today.

Just to the north of the aforementioned sits the magnificent Italian Renaissance styled church, St. Paul's.

This church stands on the site of the first Roman Catholic Church ever built in Toronto back in 1822. It is well worth your time to pay a visit to this church regardless of your religious denomination just to see the interior, it is absolutely beautiful.

At the foot of Power, on King Street, number 417 to be exact, stands the oldest surviving church in the City of Toronto. It was built in the year 1843 right in the heart of the Irish Protestant community. It kind of had two names, one of those names was "The Poorman's Church" but it's real name was, as it is known today, Little Trinity Church.

By the way, this church is a real architectural masterpiece.

Taking a short stroll down Trinity Street till you arrive at 106, you stop and stare at what looks like an old stable or a old-style garage, or even maybe a blacksmith's shop, but it is neither, it is listed as a school. That's right, a school.

This building was erected in the year 1848 by a wealthy Torontonian by the name of Enoch Turner, and it was so named the Enoch-Turner Schoolhouse. It was the first free school in the history of Toronto.

As you walk east along King you come to a halt at Sackville and as your eyes look southward they fall upon a solid looking building that sits back from the corner of Eastern avenue on the east side of Sackville. The corner-stone tells you that it was built in 1887 and the sign on the wall tells you that it is Sackville Street School, public.

Crossing over to the north side of King you walk along until you arrive at the corner of Bright and King and there you are looking at a building that has been painted a very bright pink color, and that they called it The Pink Church. It was later re-named the King East United and became very well known for it's great humanitarian work among the people in the district, along with some of the city's great basketball teams that played under the banner—King East.

Turning up Sumach we stop at the indestructible Dixon Hall. This small building has been housing giants among the under-priviledged workers for countless years. Their outstanding work and benevolence among the city's east-end indigents and problem-people is monumental.

Looking eastward at Queen and Sumach we watch a young paraplegic, Robert Pigeon, bring his newspapers to his little booth that stands by itself on the north-east corner and awaits for his first customer. Bobby carried out this daily routine for many many years, and in all types of weather.

As you look to your left your vision comes in contact with the old Dominion Brewery Hotel that stands on the north-east corner of Queen and Sumach. To the immediate west of the hotel stands the concern that feeds their child, for it is the daddy of them all—the Dominion Brewery."

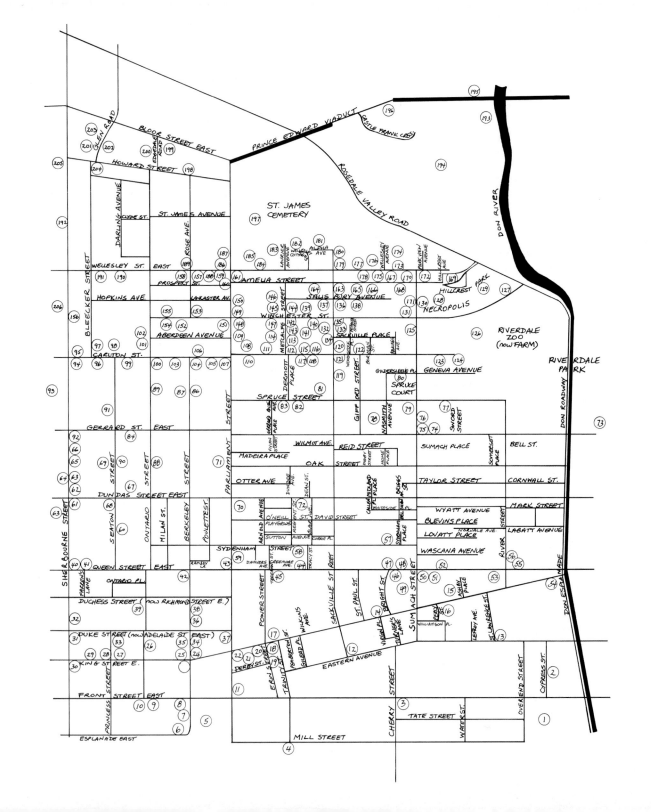

A Self-Guided Walking Tour Through Cabbagetown And Vicinity

* The letters "A", "C", or "H" or any combination of them indicate that the building is on the Toronto Historical Board's list of buildings of significance:

"A"—Listed for architectural reasons
"C"—Listed for contextual reasons
"H"—Listed for historical reasons

Dates and the names of architects are shown if known. More than one date denotes changes. The numbers correspond to those on the map. The "tour" begins at the south-east part of the area and proceeds east and west on cross-streets from south to north.

1. 145 Front Street East, Wm. Davies Meat-packing, 1860-5, C.
2. 1-37 Cypress Street, Wickett and Craig, tanners, (originally Bickell and Wickett), c. 1888.
3. SW Front and Cherry Streets, Palace Street School, 1859, Joseph Sheard; 1906, Cherry Street Hotel, AC.
4. Trinity Street, Gooderham and Worts Complex; 1859, 1870's, David Roberts, ACH.
5. Site of First Government Buildings of Upper Canada, 1794-7 until 1813; rebuilt 1820, burned 1824.
6. 2 Berkeley Street, Toronto Knitting and Yarn Factory, 1868, C.J. Gibson, with later additions, AH.
7. 24-6 Berkeley Street, Consumers' Gas Co. buildings, 1886-92, Strickland & Symons, AC.
8. 251 Front Street East, Consumers' Gas Co. building, 1887, Strickland & Symons, AC.
9. 223 Front Street East, Standard Woollens Mills, 1882, E.J. Lennox; 1893; 1899; AC.
10. 219-221 Front Street East, Leadley and Barber Woollen Mills, 1885, AC.
11. 45 Parliament Street, Consumers' Gas Co. building, 1898, 1904, Bond & Smith, AC.
12. Sackville Street Public School, 1887, Wm. G. Storm, AH, THB plaque.
13. Wall painting—'The History of the Scrap Metal Business', 1977, by Uldis Gailis, commissioned by Leon Kominsky, Canada Iron & Metals.
14. NW King and Sumach Streets, King Street East Methodist Church, 1903.
15. Ashby Place, (all houses), 1890, A.
16. Percy Street, and four houses on King Street East, 1880's.
17. 362-4 King Street East, 1874, Robert Paul, builder.
18. SW King and Trinity Streets, Little Trinity Church, 1843, Henry Power Lane, 1878; Bower Langley, Langley & Burke, 1887; Darling & Curry, ACH, Prov. Plaque.
19. Trinity Street, Enoch Turner Schoolhouse, 1848, ACH, Prov. Plaque.
20. 417 King Street East, Little Trinity Rectory, 1853, AC.
21. 399-403 King Street East, c. 1855, ACH.
22. 393-7 King Street East, Derby Tavern, 1846-7.
23. 359 King Street East, Kemi Corp. building, 1891, C.
24. 302 King Street East, Garbaldi House Tavern, c. 1860, altered 1872, C.
25. 298-300 King Street East, (#300 was J.H. Greenshields, General Store), 1875, AC.
26. 15 Ontario Street, Drug Trading Co., 1947-8, (an example of late Art Moderne architecture).
27. 256 King Street East, c. 1890, AC.
28. 252 King Street East, store, AC.
29. 236 King Street East, 1889, C.
30. 249 King Street East, Grand Central Hotel, 1868, altered 1905, Henry Simpson, A.
31. 363-5 Adelaide Street East, 1848, Paul Bishop, builder.
32. Sherbourne Street, east side north from Adelaide, factory of Gerhard Heintzman Pianos; wall advertising can still be seen on both buildings.
33. 419 Adelaide Street East, 1860's, site of "Toronto Electric Company". (demolished)
34. 55-79 Berkeley Street, row housing, 1872. C.
35. 70 Berkeley Street, No. 4 Firehall 1905, City Architect, AC.
36. 95 Berkeley Street, Christie Brown stables, 1906.
37. SW Parliament and Adelaide Streets, Pioneer Carriage & Wagon Works, c. 1891.
38. 111-113 Berkeley Street, houses, 1881-2, AC: 115 Berkeley Street, 1872, later front gable, C.
39. SW Richmond and Ontario Streets, factory of Gendron Industries Ltd., c. 1892.
40. 216-232 Queen Street East, 1889, AC.
41. 234-242 Queen Street East, Carlisle Block, 1892-3, AC.
42. 315 Queen Street East, Berkeley Street Methodist Church, 1871, Smith & Gemmell, AC.
43. NW Queen & Parliament Streets, "The Elephant & Castle, later Rupert's Hotel, c. 1878.
44. NW Queen & Tracy Streets, Imperial Theatre, later Rialto Theatre, now Good Shepherd Refuge.
45. SE Queen & Power Streets, St. Paul's Roman Catholic Church, 1887, Joseph Connelly, ACH.
46. 467-477 Queen Street East, Davies Terrace, 1877.
47. 468 Queen Street East, Dominion Brewery, 1879-80, AC.
48. 498 Queen Street East, Dominion House, 1889-91, A.
49. 58 Sumach Street, Dixon Hall, est. 1929.
50. SE Queen & Sumach Streets, Freyseng Cork Co., c. 1889.
51. 491-497 Queen Street East, terrace row, 1886, AC.
52. 524-534 Queen Street East, Fee's Terrace, 1884, AC.
53. 535 Queen Street East, Carhartt Hamilton

& Co., est. 1912.

54. Queen Street East at the Don, former site of Don Station, 1881, now at Todmorden Mills.

55. NW Queen & River Streets, (behind #19 River Street) Don Brewery buildings.

56. 19 River Street, Queen City Vinegar Co., Ltd., 1905.

57. 440 Shuter Street, Park Public School, 1915-17, C.H. Bishop, AC.

58. 383 Shuter Street, narrowest house in Toronto, c. 1885-90.

59. 221-3 Parliament Street, 1872-3, AC.

60. 91 Seaton Street, 1865, AC.

61. SE Sherbourne & Dundas Streets, All Saints Church, 1874, R.C. Windeyer, AC.

62. 241 Sherbourne Street, "Allendale", home of Enoch Turner, c. 1858, ACH.

63. 230 Sherbourne Street, 1871, A.

64. 260-262A Sherbourne Street, 1890, Knox & Elliott, AC.

65. 249 Sherbourne Street, James Small house, 1858, AC (renovated as headquarters of heritage award-winning Dundas Sherbourne housing development, Diamond & Myers, 1974-5).

66. 279-285 Sherbourne Street, AC.

67. 358-62 Dundas Street East, 1867, and 364-8 Dundas Street East, 1875, A.

68. 136-140 Seaton Street, Wm. Hall, builder, 1860, AC.

69. 208-210 Seaton Street, A.

70. 309 Parliament Street, Bluebell Theatre.

71. Plaque: "The Dufferin City School 1876" on Lord Dufferin School.

72. 509 Dundas Street East, St. Bartholomew's Church, 1888-9.

73. Don Jail, 1858, William Thomas, ACH.

74. 438-446 Gerrard Street East, 1885-8, A.

75. 436 Gerrard Street East, grocery store, later Avion Hotel, 1890-1, AC.

76. 289 Sumach Street, Ontario Medical College for Women, 1889, attrib. Smith & Gemmell, ACH, THB plaque.

77. 119-133 Spruce Street, terrace row, 1887, Thomas Bryce, builder, AC.

78. Site of Toronto General Hospital, 1855-1914, William Hay, (demolished 1921) THB plaque.

79. SW Sumach & Spruce Streets, Gerrard Street Methodist Church, 1923, now Gerrard Kiwanis Boys and Girls Club.

80. NW Sumach & Spruce Streets, Spruce Court Apartments, 1913, Eden Smith, 1926 Mathers & Haldenby, ACH.

81. 56 Spruce Street, 1872, A.

82. 41 Spruce Street, Trinity Medical School, 1871, ACH, THB plaque.

83. 35 Spruce Street, c. 1861.

84. Gerrard Street south side between Ontario & Berkeley Streets, Girls' Home, c. 1871-2.

85. 365-9 Berkeley Street, 1880's.

86. 371-391 Berkeley Street, 1880's-1905, (all listed AC).

87. 376 Berkeley Street, 1882-3, AC.

88. 349 Ontario Street, Central Neighbourhood House, (est. 1911).

89. 441 Ontario Street, the "Black House".

90. 231 Seaton Street, 1869, Wm. Dudley, builder, A.

91. 306 Seaton Street, 1863, A.

92. 291 Sherbourne Street, "Culloden", home of John Ross Robertson, c. 1881, AH, Prov. plaque.

93. Palm House, Allan Gardens, 1908, R. McCallum, AC, Prov. plaque.

94. SE Sherbourne & Carlton Streets, Sherbourne Street Methodist Church, 1876, Langley & Burke, AC.

95. NE Sherbourne & Carlton Streets, Sacred Heart Church, 1936-9, J. Gibb Morton.

96. 165-179 Carlton Street, "Chamberlin Block", 1877, Charles Chamberlin, builder.

97. NE Carlton & Bleeker Streets, St. Peter's Anglican Church, 1865, Gundry & Langley, AC, THB plaque.

98. 192 Carlton Street, house of A. McLean Howard, 1850, 1910, AC.

99. 181-3 Carlton Street, 1878, Charles Chamberlin, builder, 1887-8, AC; 185 Carlton Street, 1860-5 AC; 187-9 Carlton Street,

1878, Charles Chamberlin, builder; 191 Carlton Street, 1892, AC.

100. 197-201 Carlton Street, 1897, J.W. Gray AC.

101. 474 Ontario Street, First Church of Christian Assoc., 1905, F.J. Bird, AC.

102. 484-490 Ontario Street, 1877.

103. 203 Carlton Street, 1883, AC; 205-207 Carlton Street, 1880-1, AC; 209-211 Carlton Street, 1872, AC; 213-215 Carlton Street, 1880, AC.

104. 219 Carlton Street, 1882, AC.

105. 229-231 Carlton Street, 1872, A.

106. 230-2 Carlton Street, 1864, AC.

107. SW Carlton & Parliament Streets, Canadian Bank of Commerce, 1905, Darling & Pearson, AC.

108. 254 Carlton Street, c. 1880.

109. 511 Parliament Street, Carlton Theatre.

110. 255-9 Carlton Street, c. 1890, Benjamin Brick, builder.

111. 258-270 Carlton Street, 1883, AC.

112. NE Carlton & Metcalfe Streets, utility hole cover dated 1889, one of many in the area.

113. 1-25 Metcalfe Street, 1885-8, (listed C or AC).

114. 20-32 Metcalfe Street, 1885, AC.

115. 280-2 Carlton Street, 1886, AC.

116. 288 Carlton Street, 1881, AC.

117. 295 Carlton Street, 1878, AC.

118. 297 Carlton Street, 1892, AC.

119. 377 Sackville Street, 1876-7, Bryce & Hagon, builders, AC.

120. 308 Carlton Street, 1890, Benjamin Brick, builder, for himself.

121. 314 Carlton Street, 1875, Benjamin Brick, builder, for himself, AC.

122. 320 Carlton Street, 1877, AC.

123. 397 Carlton Street, 1883, AC.

124. 419-421 Carlton St. 1883, AC.

125. 384 Sumach St., "Witch's House", 1866, AC.

126. Riverdale Park and Farm, formerly Riverdale Zoo (1894-1974); Donnybrook Pavilion, 1902, AH; Pennsylvania-style barn, 1858's; Napier Simpson House, 1977,

Napier Simpson AC; small farm, 1977, Napier Simpson, THB plaque.

127. Site of Don Vale House tavern, 1840's -1875-76.

128. Necropolis Cemetery, laid out, 1858; chapel and gate house, 1872, Henry Langley, ACH; crematorium, 1933, J.F. Brown and Son.

129. Grave marker of William Lyon Mackenzie.

130. Grave markers of Samuel Lount and Peter Matthews.

131. 156 Winchester St., house of Daniel Lamb, 1830-40, 1867, 1877, ACH.

132. 384-386 Sackville St., 1891, AC.

133. Flagler St., (all houses), 1889, AC.

134. 407-409 Sackville St. 1889, AC.

135. 419-421 Sackville St. 1889, C; 423 Sackville St., 1889-90, AC.

136. 435 Sackville St., (rear), house of John Eastwood, 1856, A.

137. 406-412 Sackville St., 1890, AC.

138. 439-441 Sackville St., 1888, AC.

139. 92-98 Winchester St., 1898, attrib. Smith and Gemmell, AC.

140. 89 Winchester St., 1884, AC.

141. 85 Winchester St., 1857, AC.

142. S.E. Winchester and Metcalfe Sts., Hampton Mansions, 1910.

143. 37 Metcalfe St., 1875, 1892, J. Wilson Gray, 1912, AC.

144. 80 Winchester St., St. Enoch's Church, 1891; later Don Vale Community Centre, then Toronto Dance Theatre, AC.

145. 36 Metcalfe St., house of William Hannah, 1852.

146. 50-52 Metcalfe St., 1899, AC.

147. 71 Winchester St., was Coronado Private Hospital, 1920's-1930's.

148. S.E. Parliament and Winchester Sts., Winchester Hotel, was the Lake View; Winchester Hall, 1881, main building, 1888, Thomas Kennedy, ACH.

149. N.E. Winchester and Parliament, Gibson Marble Works, c. 1890.

150. 547 Parliament St., Gibson Marble, Flint Medical Glass, Essentials Garments, Bobbins Restaurant.

151. 502-8 Parliament St., 1879, J. Bowden, builder, A.

152. 21 Winchester St., home of Rev. Samuel Boddy, 1863.

153. 1-11 Rose Ave., 1879, (except for #5, a recent replica), AC.

154. 13-19 Winchester St., 1878-1880, AC.

155. Winchester Public School, 1897, 1901, AC, THB plaque.

156. 437 Sherbourne St., house for Rev. Alex Sutherland, (in 1974, it was the Playmate Club, body-rub parlour), 1878, AH.

157. 45-47 Rose Ave., 1877, AC.

158. 56 Rose Ave., c. 1858, 1878.

159. 38 Prospect St., 1878, AC.

160. 576 Parliament St., Nettleship's Hardware, 1876.

161. N.E. Parliament and Amelia Sts., Barr's Dairy, 1889, AC.

162. 36-40 Amelia St., 1873, AC.

163. 459-461 Sackville St., 1888, AC.

164. 12-22 Salisbury Ave., 1889-93, AC.

165. 46 Salisbury Ave., 1887, C.

166. 62-82 Salisbury Ave., 1889, C.

167. 126-128 Amelia St., 1878, AC.

168. 127-135 Amelia St., 1876, AC.

169. Hillcrest Park—site of P.R. Lamb Manufactory, 1848-1888.

170. 132-136 Amelia St., 1881, AC.

171. 410-412 Sumach St., 1884, AC.

172. 442-456 Sumach St., 1886, AC.

173. 423 Wellesley St., E., 1888, Knox and Elliott, A.

174. Wellesley Ave., (all houses), 1887, AC.

175. 414-428 Wellesley St. E., c. 1888, C.

176. 402½ Wellesley St. E., the "Owl House", house for Charles W. Jefferys, 1893-4, Charles T. Jefferys, builder.

177. 398-402 Wellesley St. E., 1883-5, AC.

178. 385-401 Wellesley St. E., 1889-90, C.

179. 376-380 Wellesley St. E., 1888, C.

180. 483-503 Sackville St., 1889-90, C.

181. Alpha Avenue, (all houses), 1887, AC.

182. Wellesley Cottages, 1886-7, AC or C.

183. Laurier Ave., (all houses), 1889, AC.

184. 314 Wellesley St. E., 1890, AC.

185. 306A and 306B Wellesley St. E., houses joined over driveway.

186. 562-566 Parliament St., "Darling Terrace", 1877, AC.

187. 568-582 Parliament St., 1876, C.

188. 273-277 Wellesley St. E., 1887, AC.

189. 257-263 Wellesley St. E., 1878, AC.

190. 205-207 Wellesley St. E., 1888, AC.

191. 199-203 Wellesley St. E., 1879, AC.

192. 520 Sherbourne St., Our lady of Lourdes Church, 1884-6, F.C. Law, A.C.

193. Sandy Point, Don River, old swimming hole.

194. Site of Castle Frank, summer home of Lt. Gov. John Graves Simcoe and Elizabeth Posthuma Gwillim Simcoe 1794, demolished 1829.

195. Prince Edward Viaduct, 1914-16, Edmund Burke, AC.

196. Historical plaque: Castle Frank, Elizabeth Simcoe, Don Valley Conservation Authority.

197. St. James Cemetery, laid out 1845, J.G. Howard, Chapel of St. James-the-Less, 1858, Cumberland and Storm, AC; family tombs listed AC by THB: Austin, Brock Gooderham, Gzowski, Howland, Jarvis, Manning and Severs; fence and gate, 1905, Darling and Pearson, AC.

198. 76 Howard St., 1887, A.

199. 1-11 Edgedale Rd., 1902, Eden Smith, AC or C.

200. 40 Howard St., Church of St. Simon the Apostle, 1888, W.L. Symons, AC.

201. 6-12 Glen Road, 1883, A. Coleman, builder, AC.

202. 9 Glen Rd., 1888, Eden Smith, AC.

203. 14-16 Glen Rd., 1888, AC.

204. 21-35 Howard St., 1875-1878, W. McBean, builder, AC.

205. 582 Sherbourne St., James Cooper house, 1880, AC.

206. 418 Sherbourne Street, St. Leonard Hotel, 1881, A.

Footnotes

1. *Cabbagetown Store,* J.V. McAree, The Ryerson Press, Toronto, 1953, p.1

2. *Cabbagetown,* Hugh Garner, The Ryerson Press, Toronto, 1968, Author's Preface

3. *Cabbage Town,* W.B. Hambly, in The York Pioneer, 1969, p. 33 at p.33

4. The first number of *The Cabbagetowner,* published by D & N Communications, May 1982, proclaims: "Cabbagetown area is that east of Sherbourne Street to the Don Valley, and from Gerrard to just north of Wellesley Street."

5. *The Diary of Mrs. Simcoe,* John Ross Robertson, William Briggs, Toronto, 1911, p. 179

6. *The Diary of Mrs. Simcoe,* ibid, p. 189

7. *Toronto, Past and Present: Historical and Descriptive,* Rev. Henry Scadding and John Charles Dent, Hunter, Rose and Company, Toronto, 1884, p. 93

8. *Toronto "Called Back", From 1897 to 1847* Conyngham Crawford Taylor, William Briggs, Publisher, Toronto, 1897, p. 35

9. *Robertson's Landmarks of Toronto,* John Ross Robertson, editor, Volume I, 1894, p. 447

10. *Cabbage Town,* op.cit. footnote 3, p. 40

11. *Dufferin School Old Boys' Association,* Year Book, Volume IV, 1931

12. *One Damn Thing after Another,* An Autobiography by Hugh Garner, McGraw-Hill Ryerson, Toronto, 1973, pp. 5-6

13. *Sunshine on Sumach Street,* A Reminiscence by Sophie Stransman, Jewish Dialog, Summer, 1978, p. 3, p. 4

14. *Cabbagetown Store,* J.V. McAree, The Ryerson Press, Toronto, 1953

15. *Illustrated Toronto, Past and Present,* J. Timperlake, P.A. Gross, Toronto, 1877, pp. 147-8

16. *History of Toronto and the County of York,* C. Blackett Robinson, publisher, 1885, Vol. I, p. 287

17. *The Changing Residential Patterns in Toronto,* 1880-1970, Kenneth Malcolm Campbell, 1970, (Thesis), p. 102

18. *Cabbagetown,* op. cit. footnote 2, pp. 6-7

19. *The Municipality of Toronto—A History,* Jesse Edgar Middleton, The Dominion Publishing Company, Toronto, 1923, Vol. II, p. 695

20. *Toronto, No Mean City,* Eric Arthur, University of Toronto Press, Toronto, 1964, p. 187

21. *Robertson's Landmarks of Toronto,* John Ross Robertson, editor, Volume IV, 1904, p. 55

22. *Centennial Story, The Board of Education for the City of Toronto* Honora M. Cochrane, Editor, Thomas Nelson & Sons, Toronto, p. 85

23. *Cabbagetown Diary: A Documentary,* Juan Butler, Peter Martin Assoc. Ltd., Toronto, 1970

24. *"Remembering the Don",* Charles Sauriol, Amethyst., Toronto, 1981, pp. 122-3

25. *Transit in Toronto,—1849-1967,* Toronto Transit Commission, 1967, p.2

26. *McIntyre v. Coote,* (1909) 21 Ontario Law Reports, 9

27. *Toronto, No Mean City,* op. cit. footnote 20, p. 140

28. *Illustrated Toronto, Past and Present,* op cit. footnote 15, p. 200

29. *Fighting Back,* Graham Fraser, Hakkert Toronto, 1972, p. 32

30. *J.F. Brown Company v. The Corporation of the City of Toronto,* (1916) 36 Ontario Law Reports p. 189; affirmed 55 Supreme Court Reports, p. 153.

BIBLIOGRAPHY

Adam, G. Mercer: *Toronto—Old and New,* The Mail Publishing Co., Toronto, 1891.

Arthur, Eric: *Toronto—No Mean City,* University of Toronto Press, Toronto, 1964.

Corelli, Rae: *the toronto that used to be,* The Toronto Star Limited, 1964.

Dufferin School Old Boys Association: Yearbooks, 1928-193? Published by Dufferin School Old Boys' Association.

Garner, Hugh: *Cabbagetown.* The Ryerson Press, Toronto, 1968.

Garner, Hugh: *One Damn Thing After Another, an Autobiography* McGraw-Hill Ryerson Limited, Toronto, 1973.

Hambly, William B: *Cabbagetown,* An Article Appearing in the York Pioneer, York Pioneer and Historical Association, 1969, p.33.

Hounsom, Eric Wilfrid: *Toronto In 1810.* The Ryerson Press, Toronto, 1970.

Jones, Donald: A Series of Articles on Toronto Subjects of Historical Interest; Toronto Daily Star, 1973—to the present.

Kealey, Greg: *Working Class Toronto at the Turn of the Century,* New Hogtown Press, Toronto, 1973.

Landscape Architecture, School Of: *River Mosaic: A Study of the Landscape Quality and Visual Character of the Lower Don Valley.* An Experience '78 report prepared by students. Department of Landscape Architecture, University of Toronto, 1978.

Mulvany, C. Pelham: *Toronto: Past and Present, A Handbook of the City* W.E. Caiger, Publisher, Toronto, 1884.

McAree, J. Vernon: *Cabbagetown Store.* The Ryerson Press, Toronto, 1953.

Middleton, Jesse Edgar: *The Municipality of Toronto—A History.* Three Volumes, The Dominion Publishing Company, Toronto, 1923.

Piva, Michael J.: *The Condition of the Working Class In Toronto, 1900-1921,* University of Ottawa Press, Ottawa, 1979.

Robertson, John Ross: *The Diary of Mrs. Simcoe, With Notes and a Biography.* William Briggs, Toronto, 1911.

Robertson, John Ross, Editor: *Robertson's Landmarks of Toronto,* A Collection of Historical Sketches of the Old Town of York, from 1792 until 1833 and of Toronto from 1834 to 1893. 6 Volumes, J. Ross Robertson, Toronto, 1894, 1896, 1898, 1904, 1908, 1914.

Robinson, C. Blackett, Publishers, *History of Toronto and County of York, Ontario.* Two Volumes, Toronto, 1885.

Rust-D'Eye, George H.: A Series of Articles on Subjects of Local Historical Interest; 7 News, Toronto's Oldest Community Newspaper 1975-1978.

Sauriol, Charles: *Remembering The Don, A Rare Record of Earlier Times Within The Don River Valley.* Consolidated Amethyst Communications Inc., Toronto, 1981.

Scadding, Henry: *Toronto of Old—Collections and Recollections Illustrative of the Early Settlement and Social Life of the Capital of Ontario.* Willing & Williamson, Toronto, 1878.

Scadding, Henry, and Dent, John Charles: *Toronto Past and Present: Historical and Descriptive, Memorial Volume.* Hunter, Rose and Company, Toronto, 1884.

Shuttleworth, E.B.: *The Windmill and Its Times, A Series of Articles Dealing With the Early Days of the Windmill.* Edward D. Apted, Printer, Toronto, 1924.

Sinclair, Gordon: *Will The Real Gordon Sinclair Please Stand Up.* McClelland and Stewart Limited, Toronto, 1966.

Spelt, Jacob: *Toronto.* Collier-MacMillan Canada Limited, 1973.

Stransman, Sophie, *Sunshine on Sumach Street, A Reminiscence,* Jewish Dialog, Summer 1978, p.3.

Timperlake, James: *Illustrated Toronto—Past and Present: Being an Historical and Descriptive Guide-Book.* Published by Peter A. Gross, Toronto, 1877.

Toronto Historical Board: *City of Toronto Inventory of Buildings of Architectural and Historical Importance.* Published by Toronto Historical Board. First Edition: 1977. Second Edition 1981. Third Edition 1984.

Many of the quotations from Cabbagetown old-timers are contained in materials kept available to the public in the local history collection of the Parliament Branch of the Toronto Public Library.

INDEX

CABBAGETOWN HISTORY PROJECT
—THOSE WHO HELPED

Blanca Abramson
Mary Agnew
Francis Arbour
Mrs. Arendt
Derek Armstrong
Mrs. J. Bailey
Nellie Bailey
Grace Baker
Ray Baker
Michael Barber
Pat Barnicott
Bob Barrett
Roy Beals
Lois Becker
James Beetham
Pat Belier
Mary Jane Bell
Myra Bloom
Barb Bodzki
Dorothy Bogden
Medea Boucher
Muriel Boyd
John Bradford
William Bremner
Mrs. G.G. Brigden
Ed Brill
Larry Brnjac
Eva Broomhall
Douglas Brown
Robin Browne
Doris Buchanan
Zora Buchanan
Eunice Bulger
Kay Burford
Raymond Burnes
Lois Mills Burnie
Evelyn Burrows
Frances Butler
Alma Byron
A.H. Caine
Yvonne Cameron
James Campbell
Canadian Audio-Visual
    Commission
Charles Carr
Margaret Carruthers
Rita Cassar
Nancy Castray
Central Hospital
Centre Francophone
Zena Cherry
Muriel Chubb
Dave Cleland
Jean Clift

Mrs. W. Climpson
Austin Clute
Mary Coady
Howard Cochrane
Cynthia Code
Joan Cohl
Bruce Colwill
Margaret Connor
Russell Cooper
Mabel Cosway
Angus Cranston
Eleanor Crawford
David Crombie, M.P.
Evelyn Cumberland
Hilary Cunningham
Muriel Currain
Connie D'Alessandro
Dino D'Alessandro
Bert Dantini
Bart Davis
William Dearling
B. Del Conte
Anita Dermer
Ulli Diemer
Margaret Dobie
Louise Doern
Helen Donaldson
Marg Donnelly
Iris Donovan
Michael Dougherty
Dorothy Drever
Thomas Duffy
Stewart & Mildred Duncan
Blanche Dunn
George Dyer
John Dyer
James Ealey
Harry Easton
Arthur Egan
Alice Elford
Diane Ellis
Rev. Norman Ellis
Mrs. R. Farnan
Evelyn Ferguson
George Ferguson
John Fierheller
Katrine Firstbrook
Mr. & Mrs. F.D. Fogarty
Laura Foskett
Don Fraser
Norman Funk
Chris Furedy
Pearl Gardiner
Ella Geddes

Veronica Geddes
Esther Gelbert
Josephine German
Janet Getten
Philip Giordano
Cecil Glover
Shawn Goetz-Jadon
Catherine Graham
Georgina Graydon
Jim Gregor
Eleanor Greig
J.D. Gretton
Mabel Griffin
F.G. Guerin
Rosemary Guinn
Gordon Hafenbrack
Wendy Haines-Pittman
Gladys Hall
William Hambly
Nancy Hanleigh
Doris Hanley
Pat Hannah
Betty Ann Hannon
Dorine Harrison
Pat Hay
W.G. Hayes
Ethel Hechter
Helen Hemsol
Hi-Fi Express
Joan Hill
Richard Hillman
Gordon Hinch
Luella Hockridge
Anne Hodgins
Bob Holmes
Jeanne Hopkins
Valerie Houle
Donald Hough
Lorraine Hovey
Sue Huggard
Gladys Hunt
Frances Hunter
Jack Hunter
Grant Hulburt
Charles Jewiss
Irene Johnson
Kerve Johnston
Sam Johnston
Mrs. W. Johnston
Sadie Jordan
Daryl Jung
Dorothy Kalvoda
Robert Kelly
A.M. Kennedy

Betty Kennedy
Gilbert Kent
Anna Kier
Mary King
Kay Kirker
Dorothy Lamb
Norah Lamberti
Dr. Langstaff
Harold Lapp
Alex Larry
Nancy Lawson
Keith Leigh
Pearl Lennon
Karen Levine
Llewellyn Lewis
Fred Libel
Marion Lint
Paul Lorefice
Norine Love
Hilda Luginbuhl
Nick Lye
Michael Lynch
Mona MacAllister
N. Macdonald
Ethel MacKie
Charlotte Maher
Mary Mahood
Mary Mallon
Ed Marges
John Marshall
Mary Marshall
Bruce Martin
Martha Martson
Dorothy Massey
Barbara Matutat
Vince McAuliffe
Harry McCarthy
James McCaw
Brian McDowell
John McFadyn
Marjorie McFarlane
Adele McGill
Mary McGuiness
Robert McIntyre
Ron McKee
Mary McKeown
Dorothy McVicar
Sally Meech
Susan Meech
Richard Meech
Gordon Melamed
Terry Mercier
Bob Miller
Reg Miller
Alfred Mills
Joyce Mino
Paul Mitchell
Mrs. J.F. Moeser
Dave Monahan
Mr. Moody
Lynda Moon
Olive Moore

Brian Morris
John Morrison
Gayle Mount
Roberta Munroe
Charles Murphy
Neighbourhood
    Information Post
Jane Newdick
Ellen Nickell
Carole Nyilassy
Lorne O'Donnell
Mrs. D. O'Gorman
Tom Oki
Howard O'Neill
Ontario Library Association
Charlie Oreskovich
Lois Owen
Mrs. John Palmer
Wilfred Parkin
Dr. Thomas Pashby
Ann Patterson
Helen Patterson
Aileen Pearce
Mary-Anne Pennington
Margaret Pentz
Kathleen Penwarden
Muriel Percy
Katherine Peterdy
John Piper
Bob Pomerantz
Kay Popham
Donna Porter
Ligaya Quiroga
Dorothy Quabach
Rosemary Ramnarine
Gloria Rankin
Pat Rayman
Jack Rath
Brad Reed
Eleanor Reid
Jeffrey Reid
Stephen Riggins
Carol Riley
Barbara Robb
Harry Rowe
Suzanne Roy
Dora Rust-D'Eye
Leslie Saunders
Shauna Saunders
Jane Scott
Peter Scott
John Sedgwick
Roman Semenowycz
Trudy Senesi
David Sewell
John Sewell
Elizabeth Sharp
Gordon Sinclair
Charles Smith
Constance Smith
Leslie Smith
Margaret Smith

Stephanie Smith
Vera Smith
May Snider
Helen Sommers
Brian Spain
Robert Stacey
Dorothy Stanley
Alf Statham
Norman Steinhaur
Betsy Stirling
Ernest Stolls
Irene Tanack
Margaret Taggart
Alice Taylor
Jackie Taylor
Ernie Totton
Fred Treacher
Mrs. D. Trenholme
Margaret Turnbull
Mrs. Thomas Upham
Rena Vaughan
Eric Vernon
Kathy Voddon
Mrs. Howard Wade
Stan Wadlow
Max Walker
Irv Walkin
Andrew Watson
Laura Watts
Don Weitz
Harold West
Clementina Whiteside
Emily Whittaker
June Wilcox
Stan Wilkins
Janet Williams
Audrey Wilson
Bertha Wilson
Jane Wingate
Susan Wiseman
Eva Wolfe
Rosemarie & Roy Wolfe
Margaret Woods
Nicholas Wright
Mary Wuerch
Peter Wylie
Marian Young
Violet Young
David Zapparoli